2 -

Maximizing Me

Maximizing Me

30 Lessons on the Journey to Self-Empowerment

Hart Cunningham

Aslan
PUBLISHING

Fairfield, CT

Aslan Publishing
2490 Black Rock Turnpike, #342
Fairfield, CT 06825
Please contact the publisher for a free catalog.
Phone: **203/372-0300**
Fax: **203/374-4766**
www.aslanpublishing.com

Library of Congress Cataloging-in-Publication Data

Cunningham, Hart, 1975-
  Maximizing me : 30 lessons on the the journey to self-empowerment / by
Hart Cunningham.
     p. cm.
  Summary: "A collection of thirty concise lessons based on the author's
maxims for success in business and personal life. Urges discipline,
determination and unified resolve in the pursuit of clear goals based on a
long-range life plan. Each lesson is augmented by a short assignment"—
Provided by publisher.
  ISBN 0-944031-99-4 (alk. paper)
  1. Success. 2. Success in business. 3. Self-help techniques. I. Title.

  BF637.S8C86 2007
  158.1—dc22
                              2006026652

Editing and book design by Dianne Schilling
Cover design by Anson Kuo
Printing by R.R. Donnelley
Printed in the USA

With awe and deepest gratitude, I most humbly dedicate this, my first book, to...

Dr. Peter Drucker

The Father of Modern Management

During my Masters studies at Claremont Graduate School, Dr. Drucker inspired me and my peers to create a new kind of community within our entrepreneurial efforts—a community of close relationships, shared ideals and personal values. His concept of community is ideal, not only for business, but for life itself.

Dr. Drucker challenged limits and liberated minds. One cannot overestimate the profound impact of his entrepreneurial inspiration. Organizations adhering to his organic management models demonstrate remarkably high stability and flexibility, and typically produce astounding growth rates.

Dr. Drucker was much more than a national treasure, he was a global visionary—one of our great Wise Men.

*"The individual is the central, rarest,
most precious capital resource of our society."*
—Dr Peter Ferdinand Drucker
1909-2005

Acknowledgments

My desire to write this book was inspired by one great advantage that I have enjoyed from birth. It is an advantage that I've never taken for granted, one that has sped me rapidly on my still-young quest through life to this point.

That advantage is my family.

I want to thank my father, Jere, who challenged me, and my mother, Madelyn, who nurtured me, and both of my audacious entrepreneur grandfathers, Chester and Jere Sr., who inspired me. And I give deepest loving thanks to my valiant grandmothers, Eugenia and Helen, who are the soul of all of us and have always centered the family. Combined, their powerful influences supercharged me. Every day, I realize how fortunate I am to have been born to such creative, hard-working, and true-hearted people.

My family exposed me to every conceivable intellectual and athletic challenge. They strived always, often by means mysterious to me, to build my sense of adventure and reward and possibility. Their ethical standard was simple: know yourself and to yourself be true, and value loyalty even above talent.

They taught me, by example, that without self-honesty, loyalty means nothing. They demonstrated that loyalty is the very bedrock of a successful life, successful family, successful business and successful civilization.

Positive reinforcement was our family norm. I was taught to climb the ladder of consistent goal-setting. If I slipped, there was no belittling reproach, only pride that I had tried and full support for my next attempt.

Our family lives by the faith that the greatest risk is taking no risk at all. In all things, they aim absurdly high, knowing that attaining goals is as much imagination as desire. From earliest childhood, they encouraged me. Win or lose, they gave me confidence supported with unconditional affection.

My family taught me that there is no shame in failure, only in not trying, of cowardice by avoidance, which sins against the sacred gift of life itself.

For these reasons and so many more, I praise the family that created me, nurtured me, inspired me, educated me, and then sent me out like a warrior of ancient times, to battle the real world of competitive life ...

and

Thank you to Aslan Publishing for recognizing the original manuscript's potential, and particularly to creative director Barbara Levine for her support, encouragement and guidance throughout the complex process that led to the book's completion. Thanks to marketing specialist Marcia Yudkin for reviewing the first draft and contributing to the back-cover text, to graphic artist Miggs Burroughs for assisting with the final cover design, and to Tara Miller for proofing the final draft.

Special recognition goes to graphic artist Anson Kuo for his bold, imaginative cover design, which conveys volumes about the journey to self-fulfillment in a single whimsical image.

Finally, thank you to Dianne Schilling for helping me to conceptualize a framework for the book, for editing the manuscript, and for designing the pages of the book.

Preface

Writing this book has been a daunting undertaking, an audacious and time-consuming attempt to translate my vision of successful living into words. It's a subject of great personal importance to me. Anything less would not have been worth the effort.

The book I planned to write is not the book I have written. I originally intended to chronicle my various business experiences and describe my stumbles and successes. However, I quickly realized that business axioms—mine, at any rate—cannot stand apart from life lessons. As I broadened that initial approach to encompass my entire worldview, the business focus gradually diminished and finally disappeared altogether. Perhaps it will become the subject of a later book.

In childhood, my tendency toward entrepreneurship was so strong as to seem almost genetic. At age nine, I ran a multi-neighborhood car washing business employing local kids. This adventurous enterprise launched a flurry of escalating business concepts that continued through adolescence and into adulthood, engendering the global family of businesses that grows and thrives under my leadership today.

I have learned many hard and often surprising lessons while building these numerous business entities. My worldview embraces corollaries from those experiences, as well as the elemental axioms of my family, the brilliant contributions of my personal hero, Dr. Peter Drucker, and the examples set by other great figures throughout history. I don't often name the sources of my inspiration in the 30 lessons that follow, but their influence abounds.

Every truly successful business is a community, a family, a home for people driven to succeed, to learn and to grow. Individuals within such communities have many roads to be explore. I offer this book in the spirit of personal discovery and the sincere hope that you will find it a valuable road map for your own epic journey.

Contents

Introduction

Your First Step

"The policy of being too cautious is the greatest risk of all."
—*Jawaharlal Nehru*

Over the years, hundreds of thousands of experiences have combined to make you the person you are. From the hour of your birth, through childhood and adolescence right up to the present moment, experience has shaped your life. A dizzying flood of events has propelled you into the present. If you are wise and determined, you can preserve the positive influences and reject the negative ones. You can become the person you want to be.

Many of your "firsts" will retain their initial impact. Few experiences imprint more deeply than the big events of childhood and young adulthood. You are so molded by these experiences that their effects seem fixed. Like deep cuts, they forever mark you. Nevertheless, you can choose to be free.

Unfortunately, some of us use early experiences as excuses for leading mediocre, unfulfilling, dysfunctional lives. We blame the problems of adulthood on parental indifference, material deprivation, birth order, frequent moves, addiction, family break-ups and the trauma of abuse. The list is long and, in some cases, heart-wrenching. But rarely are the effects of past events insurmountable.

While some people spend years in analysis learning to deal with past events, the overwhelming majority of people, unable to afford the time or expense of therapy, push ahead with the help of friends, family and the force of their own will. To varying degrees they manage to thwart the negative effects of the past.

In this book, I will ask you to strike a compromise. Concentrate on the present and the future, but at the same time acknowledge the events that brought you to this point. Effective teachers introduce new learning topics by starting where the students are at. In mastering your future, you need to do the same. Start with the person you are today. Understand your talents, strengths, weaknesses, habits and values by recognizing the events that shaped them.

You must take a long, hard look at yourself. You can't begin the path to self-empowerment without going through an X-ray-like process that shows where you are and where your limits are. Like a recovering alcoholic, you have to learn to see yourself as you really are. Development is a voluntary process. You must make a positive decision to take the right steps, and it starts with introspection.

You came naked into this world, and you will leave naked. But you will leave behind a legacy, the one you fashioned yourself, through your own self-invention. With the help of family, friends, learning and work, you have been inventing of yourself for as long as you have been alive, and the effort has produced the person you presently are. If you are completely satisfied with yourself at this moment, put this book down and don't waste further time. However, if you know that you would be happier if you were able to reinvent your appearance, your character, your personality, or your influence on others, then take courage from that knowledge. Make a pact with yourself to fight for maximum fulfillment of your potential.

Think about the pivotal moments in your life—your "firsts" and other significant events. You probably don't remember your first tooth, first step, or first word, but you may recall your first playmate or pet. Most of us remember our first school and teacher, our first romantic crush and first kiss. Recall your first major disappointment and your first experience with death. Remember the sadness, confusion or humiliation. Think about the excitement of graduations, cultural coming-of-age celebrations, your first job and your first experience with adult love.

Make a list of the important moments in your life. Examine each one and try to determine how it colors your outlook, personality and values today. There are no right or wrong conclusions to this exercise. The objective is to know yourself more intimately so that you can embark on the journey ahead with greater self-awareness and assurance.

When you identify qualities in yourself that you don't like (we all have them), realize that they are not necessarily your fault. Many of them were developed through repeated exposure to outside influences. Identify the source of characteristics you'd like to change, but don't dwell on them. The objective is to understand yourself, not wallow in the sea of regret.

The expression, "start with a clean slate," means to begin in a clear state of mind, set upon action. It does not mean rejecting everything about yourself and trying to become fresh as a newborn babe. That is impossible. The past cannot be wiped away. Instead, work hard to find the best in yourself and keep it. List your strengths and good qualities (more about that in the second lesson). They are the elements that make you stronger. List your negative qualities, too. Be aware that these tendencies will weaken your efforts unless you defeat them or find ways around them. Turn the page, yes. Evolve, yes. But never dismiss the crucible of forces that forged you up until now. They are the hard-earned, invaluable tools of development.

You will encounter many societal pitfalls. All around you, people will see you as you were. Some of these people will resent your attempt to better yourself. Sadly, you may experience this kind of reaction from close friends, or even family members. Painful as it is, you must proceed without the blessing of these false friends. Their envy should never hold you back.

I will help you to achieve your most highly-evolved self. If you define it realistically and are dedicated, this level of excellence is attainable. It is more than an ideal. It is a condition of personal unity leading to the realization of a personal dream— the dream you harbor deep inside of the life you want to lead, the person you want to be. That dream *can* be reached by achieving a series of carefully chosen goals and through very hard work backed by disciplined self-evaluation.

Achieving your maximum potential, as with all great and worthy struggles, will involve doubt, fear and frustration. However, it will also bring redemption. In the process you will train yourself to recognize and summon your own resolve, adjust your course with canny accuracy, and live a full, balanced life every step of the way.

To accomplish this and all the other critical tasks in this book, the central key is your fully-engaged will, your instinct for overcoming obstacles. At times you may need to persevere as though your life depended on it—because it does. The life you dream of is entirely in your hands.

When you make the decision to begin, all of your inner resources must unite to give you every possible advantage. This book will help you identify those. Using the methods outlined, you must weld them together into a single cohesive power. They will become your armada. Within you, divided and underdeveloped, is all the power you need to fuel the journey toward your goals and, ultimately, your unique vision of life. In the process you will achieve a new self—your highest self, your maximum capability.

No one can live your life for you. No one can make the journey to self-empowerment for you. And yet, if you embark on this adventure, if you tough it out and persevere, you and everyone in your circle of life will benefit enormously. If you see it through without quitting, you will enjoy these rewards for the rest of your life.

Time is precious— a tidal force at your back. There is not a moment to lose.

1

Reinvent Your Identity

"Everyone has the obligation to ponder well his own specific traits of character. He must also regulate them adequately and not wonder whether someone else's traits might suit him better. The more definitely his own a man's character is, the better it fits him."
—*Cicero*

What exactly is *identity*? In dictionary parlance, identity refers to the behavioral and personal characteristics that make a person recognizable to others. When a salesclerk asks to see an ID, most of us automatically reach for our driver's license. There we are, reduced to less than seven square inches—name, address, age, height, hair and eye color, and photographic likeness. The salesclerk looks at the license and then at us and is satisfied that we are who we say we are. Over and over again, this familiar ritual confirms our identity to a world of strangers.

Some people view identity in genealogical terms. I've met individuals who can't wait to tell me that they are descendants of some great civil war general or framer of the U.S. Constitution. Obviously they link their identity to these famous people, but what if, despite frequent reminders, no one else does?

Many of us have a secret sense of ourselves, a romanticized version that we nurture in private. At heart, we are frustrated actors, artists, PGA golfers, and skating champions. The dreams stirring in the background play a significant role in how we see ourselves, but how much do they actually affect our identities? I'm sure that I have an entirely different notion of some people than they have of themselves. Is theirs more valid than mine? Would they be justified in saying, "No, you have me all wrong?" Maybe that's what teenagers are talking about when they tell their parents, "You just don't understand me!"

Philosophers and psychologists have numerous theories relating to personal identity, theories that attempt to answer difficult questions about the existence and persistence of identity over time. Have you ever looked at an old photograph of yourself and silently wondered, "Am I still that person?" While you cannot change *numerically* (you are always the same "one"), you can certainly change *quantitatively*, through dramatic events, religious conversions, illness, losing your memory, or simply the growth of your personality. When people describe a traumatic or momentous event in their lives, they often report that they are "not the same person" they were before the event occurred.

The point I wish to make here is that you do not have to wait for external events to transform your identity. You can do it yourself—starting now. You can become the author of that *qualitative* aspect of your identity. In fact, you can design it any way you wish.

Much of this book revolves around the importance of setting and attaining goals. Goals are closely linked with who you believe yourself to be. If you set goals that are not congruent with your identity—with how you see yourself and, to some extent, how others see you—your prospects of reaching those goals will be handicapped. Conversely, if your goals do not help you to strengthen the identity to which you aspire, the person you wish to become, they are the wrong goals.

So before you venture much further in this book, take some time to examine your present identity and think about how you might want to change it. What attributes make you unique? How do you presently see and define yourself? How do others see and describe you?

Most of us receive continuous feedback from the people around us. Even if they don't verbalize their impressions, the information is conveyed through their attitudes and behaviors. All we have to do is pay attention and read between the lines. For example, maybe the reason people seldom seek your opinion is that you pontificate, or have rigid views, or are a poor listener. Conversely, maybe the reason people won't leave you alone is you've made them dependent, or you're a pushover, or an extremely good listener. Ask your friends and associates to be honest with you. Don't be defensive. If you convince them that you are open to candid feedback, most people will share their impressions.

A strong, congruous identity breeds confidence, and confidence fuels work, perseverance and, in time, success. Further, each success builds greater confidence. If your identity is that of a determined, goal-driven person, you will strive to create and maintain that reality.

Strive for a unified identity. If you harbor undefined conflict, some sharp internal division, it will affect your goals by weakening your ability to achieve and maximize personal power. Internal division can undermine all your efforts. The ensuing struggle is similar to family members feuding. They are not a team. They pull apart instead of together.

Division is always a weakness, an impediment to success in realizing goals. Concentrate on areas where you sense division. Pay attention when part of you is saying one thing and another part is urging something else, or when two powerful desires are in conflict. You can't become a concert pianist if you hate to practice. You will probably never own the home of your dreams if you spend every dime instead of saving.

Your final, collective identity will be revealed in the eulogies delivered at your funeral or the obituary printed in the newspaper. How do you want them to read? Start now to build a powerful unity of purpose. Once you look intently at your identity and find your true center, you will begin to see how identity affects all your personal goals, how it widens or limits your progress.

Identity is not a prison. With hard work, identity can evolve, just as with great effort goals can be attained. As you keep moving forward, your sense of identity will strengthen. The "you" you believe in and cherish most dearly will be realized.

Remember this ...

- **Examine your present identity.**

- **Learn how others see you.**

- **Strive for congruence between goals and identity.**

- **Eliminate internal division.**

Try this ...

Locate two photographs of yourself—a recent one and one taken during an earlier stage of your life. Go back all the way to childhood if you like. Recall the activities that you were engaged in around the time the earlier photo was taken. Then write a short description of that earlier you. What was important to you? How did you spend your time? What about your relationships with others? Next, write a similar description to go with the recent photo. Finally, write a description of the future you—the one you hope to become. Include similar details. If you like, doctor a second recent photo to show the future you, or use an image of someone else who has the physical qualities you hope to attain. Compare the three images and descriptions and note the evolving reinvention of your identity.

2

Know Your Strengths and Talents

"Hide not your talents, they for use were made. What's a sun-dial in the shade?"
—*Benjamin Franklin*

One of the exciting things about embarking on a new venture is experiencing the combustion that occurs when your unique strengths and talents are ignited by the challenge at hand. The energy produced is unlike any other in the world, because no one else in the world possesses your formula of abilities.

Your strengths are the things that you do best, the exemplary parts of your makeup, the knowledge at your immediate disposal and the skills that you have mastered. When a strength that you possess is needed by a group, people automatically turn to you. When you are performing out of strength, you feel confident and self-assured.

Talent is a little different. Talents are innate qualities that are difficult to acquire through education or training. We usually think of talent as a mysterious gift bestowed on artists, athletes and musicians. But everyone is talented in one way or another—star performances are not required. Maybe you possess an innate ability to nurture others, listen compassionately, inspire action, mediate conflicts, or articulate ideas. Perhaps you have a talent for precision, or for grasping the big picture. Talents like these can be applied in many arenas, not just on the job.

One way to discover your strengths and talents is to ask the people you live and work with to tell you what they have observed. You may be surprised to learn that the things people identify are not directly related to your assigned role. For example, a woman who was hired to do the bookkeeping at a small environmental company contributed far more as a free-floating troubleshooter because of her incredible ability to spot problems in the making and generate resources nobody knew existed. She made these contributions so effortlessly and joyfully that she was scarcely aware of doing so. But her colleagues noticed.

Another way to discover your strengths and talents is to look at your successes and identify the qualities that helped you achieve them. Try to look beyond the obvious. For example, a successful salesperson owes his high volume, not to the sophisticated repertoire of selling techniques he learned in school, but to his talent for relating to people. And a stockbroker, though she knows the markets inside-out, is admired most for her uncanny prescience regarding global economic patterns.

Once you've identified your strengths and talents, utilize them to the fullest. Find ways to capitalize on them in your work and personal life. Most of us spend too much time worrying about our weaknesses. That time could be better spent contributing from our strengths. Above all, don't waste time trying to "fix" yourself. That's a mistake lots of managers make. They put the wrong person in a job and then try to force the person to be someone they're not, frustrating everyone in the process. Be wiser than that in managing yourself. Find projects and jobs that suit your strengths and talents from the outset. In the right job, work becomes play.

Another way to use your strengths and talents is by sharing them with others through various forms of collaboration. When two professional trainers, one a gifted facilitator and the other a reservoir of technical knowledge, began to co-train, they couldn't keep up with the demand for their popular workshops. Separately they each lacked vital abilities, but together they formed an unbeatable combination.

As you proceed from goal to goal, you will learn where your greatest strengths lie. The relative effectiveness of your talents will emerge. Your strengths are the truth, the rock upon which you will build your Maximum Me.

Remember this ...

- Inventory your strengths and talents.

- Ask others how they perceive your abilities.

- Identify the qualities that helped you achieve previous goals.

- Look beyond the obvious.

- Find projects and jobs that require your strengths and talents.

- Focus on strengths, not weaknesses.

Try this ...

Think back to your childhood. Recall specific school and non-school events in which you performed or participated. What did your peers look to you for? Did they expect you to solve problems, provide leadership, amuse them, win games, be the first to try new things? What did adults expect of you? What did they say about your abilities? The talents you demonstrated in childhood are probably still with you today.

3

Stimulate, Educate and Empower Your Mind

"I think, therefore I exist."
—Descartes

Your mind is your private planet, your exclusive inner cosmos. Its mysteries are legendary. Once scientists believed that we were born with a limited number of brain cells. Now we know that the brain is highly plastic and capable of rewiring itself. With about 100 billion neurons, each of which connects with thousands of other neurons, the brain can actually generate new cells, and can redesign and enlarge its functions.

You are either exercising your brain, or stimulating it. Exercise is doing something you already know how to do. If you are a skilled tennis player, each game exercises your brain as well as your body. If you are an experienced salesperson, each selling opportunity refines your persuasive abilities. Like walking paths that are etched clearer and wider with each trip, neural pathways in your brain become stronger and more efficient with repeated use. That's why a speech is so much easier to give the fifth time than it was the first.

Doing something *new* stimulates the brain. When you study a foreign language or learn to play a song on the guitar, you are stimulating your brain to create new pathways. Thousands of neurons in different parts of the brain may be involved. Your brain rewires itself with each new learning experience. The key to getting smarter is to grow more connections between brain cells. It's these connections that allow you to solve problems and become truly skillful in any area you choose.

Stimulate your brain through reading, taking courses, listening to fine music, attending plays and engaging in dialogue with thoughtful, intelligent people. Read all kinds of things. Don't restrict recreational reading to one or two genres. Maybe you're a big fan of science fiction, mysteries, political thrillers or sports stories. Fine. But remember, if you don't branch out, your brain won't either. Add books and articles on globalization, history, world religions, brain science, astronomy and environmental issues. Enjoy poetry, biographies and the classics. Equip yourself to think deeply and converse intelligently about many subjects.

Read materials directly related to your goals. This is especially critical. For example, if one of your goals is to lose weight, subscribe to two or three magazines or newsletters on nutrition. Choose reputable publishers who dispense accurate research-based information rather than sell products. If your goal is to write a novel, read books about fiction writing, character development and publishing. Learn everything you can about the craft of writing.

Don't zone out in front of TV. The overwhelming bulk of television programming is mindless and mind-numbing. Much of it is also tasteless, crass and uncivil. It is aimed at the lowest common denominator—the minimum you, not the maximum. Even if you have hundreds of channels to choose from, the most you can ever be with TV is a passive observer. Instead, find something or someone to interact with—puzzles, games, lectures, museums, seminars, classes, book clubs, political forums, online discussion groups. The possibilities are endless.

Understand how your emotional brain works and strive to increase your emotional intelligence. Virtually every response you make to events in your environment involves an interplay of the emotional and cognitive parts of your brain. Often the emotional brain reacts first and faster than the reasoning brain, which is why emotions sometimes get out of control. Angry outbursts and debilitating fear are examples of what happens when the rational, reasoning brain fails to subdue the fight-or-flight responses of the emotional brain.

Nourish your brain by eating a healthful diet. Avoid sedating or artificially stimulating it with alcohol and other drugs. Your brain is about two percent of your body's weight, but consumes about 20 percent of its energy in the form of oxygen, nutrients and water supplied by the blood. Eight gallons of blood every hour pass through your brain. This disproportionate energy consumption speaks to the brain's dominant role in your life and requires no conscious control, but many things that affect the brain are within your control and require wise management.

You can build intellectual strength even if you have physical limitations. Actor Christopher Reeve used his mental abilities to produce good in the world right up until the day he died. Stephen Hawking has been called the most brilliant theoretical physicist since Einstein. If near total paralysis didn't stop them, why should temporary, or even chronic, disabilities stop you?

If you believe you are incapable, slow or stupid, you will be. If you accept your present level of intelligence, you are sleepwalking through life.

A common roadblock to intellectual growth is conformity. I've met numerous people who routinely sacrifice thinking and learning in an effort to fit in. If their friends spend the weekend drinking beer and watching football, they acquiesce, even though they'd rather read a book or visit a museum. Conformity is okay for teenagers, but is a great enemy of adults. You will never achieve your maximum potential by submerging your identity within a group.

Strive for unity of mind, spirit, and body. Develop all three, and keep raising the bar higher and higher. Free your mind and your life will follow.

Remember this...

- Your brain "rewires" itself with each new experience.

- Exercise your brain by practicing existing skills.

- Stimulate your brain by learning something new.

- Read, take courses, listen to music, visit museums, attend plays.

- Engage in dialogue with thoughtful, intelligent people.

- Read materials directly related to your goals.

- Build emotional intelligence.

- Nourish your brain, avoiding artificial stimulants and sedatives.

Try this ...

Create an imaginary Board of Directors consisting of real or fictional characters, living or historical. Ask your board for advice concerning important matters. Here's how it works: First, decide from whom you would like to get advice—a former president or cabinet member, your great-grandmother, a specific poet or musician. Choose at least three. Next, learn enough about your board members to know how they think and what they value. Once you feel that you understand them well enough to imagine their thought processes, begin to "consult" them regarding important decisions and problems. Ask yourself, "What would Abe tell me to do?" or "How would Abigail handle this?"

Maintain a Continuous Flow of Energy

"Energy is the essence of life. Every day you decide how you're going to use it by knowing what you want and what it takes to reach that goal, and by maintaining focus."

—*Oprah Winfrey*

We regularly draw upon four wellsprings of energy: mental, emotional, physical and spiritual. By maximizing all four sources and welding them into one, we greatly enhance our ability to achieve our goals.

Mental energy is the intellectual ability and creative will to accumulate knowledge, develop skills, make decisions and solve problems. A scientist measures mental energy in depth of problem-solving ability.

Physical energy is the body's ability to do work and to recover quickly for the next effort. A pro athlete measures physical energy in watts per hour, in weight lifted, or in velocity attained.

Emotional energy drives our desires, affections and fears, and fuels our will. The psychologist measures emotional energy as stability under stress.

Spiritual energy is a central sense of being and strength of purpose in life. We measure spiritual energy by the faith we maintain in our view of life and by the consistency of our purported beliefs and deeds.

In highly effective people, these four streams of energy are like powerful tributaries joining a great river. Although the origin and nature of each is different, upon merging they become indistinguishable —a unified flow of pure energy. Not much can stand in the way of such a great river.

In order to actualize your maximum potential, you must consolidate your energy and reach a state of complete agreement within yourself. Nothing within you can hold back. All of your resources must work in concert. Consolidated energy allows you to experience your goals with your entire being. Instead of merely thinking about and verbalizing your goals, you feel them, demonstrate them, and believe deeply in them.

Feeling your goals means strongly desiring them, being enthusiastic about them and celebrating the image of yourself achieving them. Thinking your goals involves analyzing the forces and factors involved, monitoring and assessing your progress and solving problems along the way. Demonstrating, or acting upon, goals is doing the physical work required—putting 100 percent effort into the tedious as well as enjoyable tasks. Having faith in your goals means believing in their worth and in your own ability to achieve them.

Marathon runners, for example, are excited by the thought of running competitively, exhilarated by the sensations, smells and sounds of hundreds of bodies pushing their limits, and emotionally committed to doing whatever it takes to finish, place or win. They research long-distance running, learn what works and doesn't, analyze past performances and use the information to set and achieve training objectives. They spend hours in regular workouts and practice runs that build speed, strength and endurance without causing injury. And finally, they believe in themselves, building the necessary spiritual strength to endure pain and exhaustion in those final arduous miles.

I came up with a formula to illustrate the relationship of energy and determination, the two main factors that I believe contribute to success. The formula is arbitrary, not based on any scientific research, but it helps me put my attention where I think it will make the most difference.

Success equals Energy times Determination squared (S = E x D^2)

In other words, consolidated energy—that river combining the four tributaries—when multiplied by determination multiplied by itself produces success. Determination in this formula is firmness of purpose, a quality that the great psychologist Rollo May called intentionality. It's the kind of wordless resolve that compels you to get up at 4:30 in the morning to jog when every fiber of your being wants to sleep another hour. It takes a river of energy to do that and the square of determination to channel that energy. When you've done your homework, preparing in every way possible to meet your goals, intentionality takes over. Energy driven by determination flows into every effort.

Energy, however, is not limitless. No one, no matter how determined, can keep going indefinitely. Energy must be recharged and renewed. Without continued replenishment, those tributaries that feed the great river will turn to trickles and eventually dry up.

Mental energy is recharged by exercising the mind—by reading, playing chess, solving problems, testing new ideas and challenging yourself to master new subjects and skills.

Emotional energy is derived by interacting with friends and loved ones, and by doing what inspires you, whether that's listening to music, playing an instrument, painting, gardening, camping, volunteering, or some other pursuit that gives you joy and satisfaction.

Physical energy is kept at peak levels by eating a healthful diet, exercising regularly and getting adequate sleep. Recreational recharging through sports and hobbies also builds physical energy.

Spiritual energy is sustained by making ethical decisions, adhering to high moral values like truthfulness, kindness, respect, responsibility, fairness and good citizenship, and by practicing your faith.

You may have heard the expression, "Take time to sharpen the saw." It's another way of describing the need to take time for yourself, time to rebuild your energy. If the carpenter neglects to sharpen his saw, the blade gradually grows dull, splinters the wood and destroys the artistry. So stay sharp. Avoid dullness. Check your energy levels regularly and keep them high.

Remember this ...

- **You produce four kinds of energy: mental, emotional, physical and spiritual.**

- **By consolidating energy from all sources, you experience your goals with your entire being.**

- **S=E x D^2 (Success=Energy x Determination^2)**

- **Regularly recharge and renew all four forms of energy.**

- **Sharpen the saw.**

Try this ...

Appraise your energy levels in all four areas. Where are your levels usually highest—mental, emotional, physical or spiritual? Where are they generally lowest? Devise plans to build energy wherever it is needed to bring the flow into balance.

5

Embrace Change

"Human beings, by changing the inner attitudes of their minds, can change the outer aspects of their lives."
— *William James*

Who you are is always changing. Nothing in your physical or mental makeup is static. Cells are discarded and rebuilt daily. Your brain rewires itself with each new learning. Your beliefs and attitudes are modified by exposure to new ideas. Your disposition darkens when things go badly and brightens when they go well. Your general outlook fluctuates from day to day, week to week, depending on world and local events. Your energy level changes based on the food you eat, the amount and quality of sleep you get and the fluctuating state of your health. A decision you make today may seem like the wrong decision tomorrow.

You are being shaped and modified by a constant barrage of outside influences, as well as by forces inside yourself. Through growth and the accumulation of knowledge and experience, you become who you are. But who you are is dynamic, reforming continuously.

Your ability to consciously change and adapt is an expression of the uniquely human talent of creativity. Were humans unable to change, we would not have survived the many cataclysmic events that have visited life on Earth.

At any age and at any stage in life, you can change. You have the power to reinvent yourself. It is a difficult road, but the results are attainable. Goal by goal, you can remake yourself into a more effective, more productive, more successful person— and a happier, better person as well. But you must want to change and want it desperately.

Ask yourself quite bluntly: Am I satisfied with who I am? Am I fortified with self-respect? Do I believe in my own worthiness? What changes do I want to make? Since your body and brain are altering daily, you might as well direct a portion of the remodeling process. You know what is good for you. Start putting together a game plan for change.

To change a habit, substitute a new behavior and practice it until it eclipses the old behavior. For example, if you have a smoking habit, go for a short walk during the times you would normally take a cigarette break. Do it religiously and enjoy breathing deeply while you exercise. Stay away from the places where people congregate to smoke.

To change an emotion, modify the thoughts that produce it. For example, if you are angry at a friend for letting you down, instead of concluding that the friend's behavior was deliberate, tell yourself it was an oversight or an unavoidable happenstance. Don't ever tell yourself that you "can't help" how you feel. In fact, you are the *only* person who can help.

To change a thought or opinion, learn more about the subject, opening yourself to other points of view. For example, if your views regarding a particular project at work are at odds with everyone else's, take some time to familiarize yourself with opposing positions. In this age of rapid change and exploding information, it's rarely smart to cast your ideas in concrete.

To change your appearance, modify your wardrobe or hair style, lose weight, build muscle tone, or gain better balance and grace by practicing Tai Chi, yoga or dance.

Remember these words: consistency and longevity. They are the most important elements of change. Consistency in this context means producing uniform performances with minimal deviation—in other words, doing the new thing the same way every time. Longevity means doing it over a long period of time.

Change takes extended effort. Drastic, short-term changes don't work. Imagine trying to go from an eight to a 16-hour work-day in one jump. How long do you think that would last? If you need to work harder, you'll fare much better by increasing work hours in small increments over many months. Similarly, if you try to lose weight on a crash diet, you will almost assuredly gain it back. Lifestyle changes—more exercise combined with a healthful diet—produce slower weight loss, but the consistency and longevity of the effort are more likely to produce lasting re-sults.

Relative affluence combined with rampant consumerism has produced an expectation of instant gratification. With fast-food beckoning from every corner and supermarket aisles stocked with high-calorie processed foods, whole countries are sinking in excess fat. In the meantime, legions of cosmetic surgeons market more instant gratification. Tell me, which would you rather do—walk around the block three times a day, or pay thousands of dollars for liposuction? People overeat because eating is their greatest pleasure. Surely there's something else they could en-joy. Why does a surgeon have to tie up their stomachs?

What does it take to learn a foreign language? Consistency and longevity. How do you become a skilled ballroom dancer? Consistency and longevity. What is the secret of successful in-vesting? Consistency and longevity of effort in every aspect of knowledge and skill required to do the job.

There are no easy answers, but take heart. Whatever path you have taken up to now, your past is not a prison. Don't be afraid to change.

I'll say it again: you have the power to reinvent yourself. Learning and assimilating this one fact will give you the key to change itself. The first decisive step is yours and yours alone. If you truly believe in your ability to change, if you truly are willing to change, nothing can stop you.

Prepare to minimize the shortcomings that shackle you and maximize the abilities that will send you soaring.

Remember this ...

- Who you are is dynamic, changing continuously.
- At any age or stage, you can reinvent yourself.
- Put together a game plan for change.
- To change a habit, substitute a new behavior.
- To change an emotion, modify the thought that produces it.
- To change an opinion, be open to other views.
- Achieve change through consistency and longevity.

Try this ...

Change can be difficult and uncomfortable, which is why many people avoid it. Every time a major change occurs in your life, you must go through a transition period as you say good-bye to the old and adapt to the new. To prepare for change, read some of the books and articles of change expert, William Bridges. His approach to managing transitions can be extremely helpful.

6

Pull Yourself Together

" Perhaps the most valuable result of all education is the ability to make yourself do the thing you have to do, when it ought to be done, whether you like it or not; it is the first lesson that ought to be learned; and however early a man's training begins, it is probably the last lesson that he learns thoroughly."

—Thomas H. Huxley

"Pull yourself together." How many times have you heard that plea? But have you ever heard it as, "Pull your SELF together?"

When a person is fragmented by disorganization, confusion, fear or doubt, it seems as if that person is literally falling apart.

We urge our children to "get it together" when they are forgetful, make foolish mistakes, earn poor grades, or behave irresponsibly. We issue ourselves the same mandate when we feel muddled or out of control. We say, "She's got it together," about someone who is orderly, poised, focused and successful.

I have business dealings with a man who needs to pull himself together. He can't remember the status of projects, mixes up people's names, doesn't complete tasks in a timely manner and always seems harried. He's been "getting organized" for years, but nothing ever seems to change.

Some people seem to prefer chaos to order, fragmentation to wholeness, division to unity. Like the employee who never seems able to find the file or document he needs and repeatedly asks colleagues to supply copies for him, or the one who rarely finishes a project on time because she continually changes direction. As a rule, fragmented people are frustratingly difficult to work with. They really do need to pull themselves together. But how?

One thing that seems to help is to get rid of external chaos. It's difficult to be unified on the inside if everything in your environment is in disarray. That applies not just to "stuff," but to people coming and going demanding your attention and making it impossible for you to focus. Straightening your office is a good place to start, but you may need to straighten your whole life.

When you're falling apart emotionally, take a time-out. Twenty minutes may be enough, or you may need a couple of hours, or days. The reasoning brain is slower than the emotional brain. Give it some time to catch up. Then sort out your emotions. Write them all down and see if you can link each one to a specific event or issue in your life. Talk to someone who is a good listener—a professional if necessary.

If your mind is darting in a hundred different directions at once, force yourself to make lists and daily plans. You wouldn't allow your dog to run pell-mell all over the neighborhood. You'd control him with a leash. Control your mind with a plan. Let the plan rein you in when you start to stray. If you don't trust yourself to stick to a plan, enlist the help of coworkers or family members. Ask them to tell you when you seem distracted or scattered.

If you feel spiritually broke, reexamine the values and sense of purpose that guide your life. Notice how many of your daily activities actually nourish your spirit. If the answer is none, get back into balance. Devote time to activities that uplift you and give you joy—camping, fishing, gardening, sailing, poetry, great music, intimacy with loved ones, religious studies.

So go ahead and fall apart. But don't "pull yourself together" until you've examined the pieces—mental, emotional, physical and spiritual. Obviously, in a state of disunity there is no wholeness, no strong central core. Under pressure you can lose your "center," the gravity that holds you together. Find out where you need to devote additional effort in the quest to become unified. Don't wait until next week, or next month, or after New Year's. Take action now.

Mind, emotions, body and spirit. Each is essential to wholeness, and all depend upon one another. Take one away and unity is lost. Without mind, spirit has no home. Without emotions, experience is colorless and bland. Without the body, life ends. Without spirit, life is pointless and empty. Yet when mind, emotions, spirit and body join in a unified concert, the full potential of human existence opens to a buffet of limitless opportunity.

Remember this ...

- Get rid of external chaos.

- Take time-outs to organize your feelings and thoughts.

- Make lists and daily plans.

- Pull your SELF together—mind, body, emotions and spirit.

Try this ...

A new category of entrepreneur has appeared in recent years: the professional organizer. These individuals have devised solutions to almost every type of fragmentation problem their grateful clients have thrown at them. Many professional organizers have written books, maintain Internet sites and write columns for newspapers and magazines. Do some checking. You'll find dozens of ideas for controlling chaos and bringing order to your life.

7

Enhance Your Reputation

"Character is like a tree and reputation like its shadow.
The shadow is what we think of it; the tree is the real thing."
—*Abraham Lincoln*

We've all heard and used expressions such as, "Your reputation precedes you," "She has a bad (or good) reputation," and "He has a reputation for being ruthless (fair, kind, crafty, a womanizer, a flirt, etc.)." Whatever you are widely reputed to be, that is your reputation. It is your external identity, the estimation in which others hold you.

Anyone who interacts with other people develops a reputation. Even people who isolate themselves build reputations—as reclusive eccentrics or hermits if nothing else.

To figure out your reputation, analyze the information you have from others. How do your family members see you? How do your associates at work perceive you? If coworkers readily confide in you, it probably means that you have a reputation for being trustworthy. If they congregate around your work station, you may be seen as congenial, entertaining or helpful. If they hit you up for frequent donations or loans, you may have a reputation as an easy mark. Open your eyes and ears and start gathering the evidence.

Evaluating your reputation can be tricky. If you happen to be a public figure, you can discern your reputation by evaluating polls, reading constituent letters and monitoring media coverage. But most of us are not public figures. Even if we muster the courage to ask a sampling of people to describe our reputation, we can't be sure that those assessments are unembellished. For one reason or another, people may be afraid to tell us the truth.

In recent years a number of companies have begun using a technique called 360-degree feedback. Employees at all levels complete feedback questionnaires for everyone in their work group, usually anonymously. Communication and relationships are often greatly improved when people find out how they are perceived by others and make positive changes accordingly.

Make a reasonable effort to assess your reputation about once a year. However, don't fall into the trap of constantly monitoring what others think of you. Preoccupation with pubic opinion can make you self-conscious at best, paranoid at worst. Besides, if you concentrate instead on developing top-notch skills and good character, reputation will take care of itself.

Overcoming a less than stellar past reputation is another matter. Reputations have a way of following us from job to job, town to town, relationship to relationship. References, recommendations, gossip and hearsay travel far and fast, and the Internet has erased any hope of keeping information contained.

Your best chance of minimizing negative carryover from a past reputation is to make a completely fresh start. If that's not possible, accept the hard path ahead. The only way to create a new reputation is indirectly, through your actions. Realize that it won't be easy. Even in today's high-speed world, reputations develop gradually. At first, people may doubt the new you.

Reputation is like a suit of clothes. If you show up wearing something very different from what people are accustomed to seeing, the new look, though novel, won't change how people perceive you. But if the new look is consistently observable, over time they will become convinced and your reputation will change.

In any case, the past is gone and cannot be changed. Instead of looking back, look ahead. The future is wide open—a blank canvas. Learn from your mistakes, but don't obsess over them. Reject any lingering guilt that continues to haunt you. Dwelling in the unchangeable past is a living death.

You can never undo past mistakes, but you can often outlive them. Build your future upon the wisdom gained from lessons hard learned. That is the brave path to personal power. Your past reputation, good, bad or mediocre, is just exactly that—past, over, done with.

A person who changes, truly changes, is redeemed from whatever life situation came before. Keep your own counsel and never falter. By reinventing yourself you can reinvent your reputation. Strive to learn from the priceless lessons of your life up to this point. Eventually, the new you will overtake the old. Consistency will redeem you.

Remember this ...

- Assess your present reputation, but don't be preoccupied with public opinion.

- Concentrate on developing top-notch skills and good character.

- Learn priceless lessons from the past.

- To reinvent your reputation, reinvent yourself.

Try this ...

Write a paragraph or two describing your current reputation as you imagine it to be. Then ask a close friend or colleague—someone your trust—to describe your reputation as he or she perceives it. Give the person a little time. Don't rush through this exercise. Finally, compare the two descriptions, keeping in mind that your reputation probably varies a bit from work to family to neighborhood, and from person to person. Decide if there is anything you want to change about your reputation and keep that in mind when setting future goals. (To get a more accurate picture, request descriptions from two or three people.)

8

See Things as They Truly Are

"Instead of thinking how things may be, see them as they are."
—*Samuel Johnson*

What exactly is "seeing?" We see the house, the car, the sidewalk, the sky, the freeway. We see our hands, our lover and the faces of our children. But do we see what is really there? Do we read the messages in the eyes of those we love? Do we comprehend their nuanced tones? Do we grasp the full meaning of their statements? Or are our deductions emotionally colored and distorted? Do any of us really see?

The question, on its surface, sounds absurd. Of course we see. And yet all of us may describe the same object in wildly different ways based to our values, assumptions, experience, and attitudes.

Jill Fredston, co-director of the Alaska Mountain Safety Center and author of *Snowstruck: In the Grip of Avalanches*, wrote this about avalanche victims in the U.S. (*New York Times*, March 11, 2006):

"... Most of those who died knew better. They had either been explicitly warned of the hazards or had enough knowledge to recognize the clues. How could some have looked at clear evidence of danger and not 'seen' it? How could others have seen the signs and overestimated their ability to deal with them?

"The trouble is that we tend to see what we expect to see, what we want to see or what we've seen before. The more we want to do something—whether it is to marry or scale a particular mountain—the more likely we are to make unchecked assumptions and pay attention only to the data that tells us what we want to hear."

Ask yourself, do you see what is really there, or what you expect, assume, or want to be there? Do your fears, doubts, opinions and desires literally reconfigure reality?

Many of us see a false world, a world shaped by the programming of childhood, rigid political and religious ideologies, and self-appointed celebrity "experts." We buy what television advertisers tell us to buy, wear the latest styles because everyone else does and decide how to vote based on 30-second sound bites.

How is it that people view various world events so differently? To one person a political cartoon is merely a statement of opinion—take it or leave it, agree with or don't. But to another it is blasphemy, a sacrilege deserving of condemnation and death.

Powerful, decisive personal energy cannot be founded on illusion. It is necessary to see clearly to develop a keen awareness of self and others. Learn to see beyond emotions and assumptions and recognize what is truly there. Be certain that what you believe is real. Identify, isolate and reject obsolete ideas and outdated emotional structures founded on prejudice, fabrication and fantasy. Many of us cling to outmoded belief systems—fond crutches from earlier days—but if they are not our own, if they have failed us, we must cut them out like cancerous tumors.

Conquer old phobias and work to overcome unfounded fears. Most people are afraid of spiders, but common household and garden spiders are completely harmless. Public speaking is said to be the number one fear of adults, but no one ever died of giving a report or presentation. Unfounded fears grow in a climate of ignorance. You can stop their growth by practicing healthy skepticism and personally investigating issues before adopting the views and beliefs of others.

In the sixth century BCE, the fearless thinker Thales of Miletus made himself known among all Greeks for his incredible intellectual ability. He calculated the weight of the pyramids and predicted eclipses. An engineer by trade, Thales was the first known Greek philosopher as well as a scientist and mathematician. He founded the Milesian school of natural philosophy, developed the scientific method and initiated the first Western enlightenment. Learned Greeks flocked to Thales for instruction and mentoring. Thales was asked by his students to name the most difficult task in a human life. Was it going to war? Raising a family? The quest for personal wealth? Facing death? Thales answered: "None of those. The most difficult quest is to know oneself."

Though the apothegm "know thyself" comes from Thales, the great teacher Jesus Christ took it much further. Jesus taught, "Know thyself and to thyself be true."

To thyself be true. How simple it sounds. With those words, Jesus gave his believers a path to unity though self-awareness. Yet, this is surely the hardest task in all human endeavor, requiring unflinching backbone and total faith. Jesus did not value easy conversions or pretense. He defended his disciple, Thomas, for having doubts.

Only by identifying false beliefs can we hope to change them. To know yourself utterly requires incredible personal courage.

Remember this ...

- Learn to see beyond emotions, assumptions and ideology.

- Recognize what is truly there.

- Conquer phobias and unfounded fears.

- Know yourself, and to yourself be true.

Try this ...

Challenge a lifelong fear, such as the fear of spiders, insects, snakes, heights, deep water, public speaking, or flying. Do it in a safe, responsible way, with the help of a professional if necessary. For example, if you are afraid of snakes, read books and visit Internet sites devoted to reptiles. Learn to distinguish poisonous from nonpoisonous snakes. Visit the reptile house at a zoo and talk with the keeper. If possible, handle a harmless snake under the keeper's supervision. If you are afraid of deep water, take swimming lessons from a licensed instructor. Gradually build up your confidence in the water. Eventually you may wish to learn snorkeling or scuba diving from a competent instructor.

9

Build a Personal Dream

"I dream, therefore I exist."
—Strindberg

Dare to dream. That phrase has become such a trite cliché, I doubt anyone really thinks about its meaning. To dare is to have courage, to do something that requires boldness. But why should dreaming require either? I'll tell you why. Because most people think that dreams are for sentimentalists and romantics—impossible to reach in the real world. And yet at the same time they recognize that a dream is an ultimate desire, a distant and magnificent vision attainable only through acts of grace or extreme effort.

Too often, people lead lives of drudgery while indulging in a secret dream life. In their fantasies they are powerful, admired and successful. They retreat to such dreams to escape the harshness of everyday life. But these are false dreams. Like heroin, they anesthetize the dreamer and make him complacent. Instead of fighting to change his circumstances, he stays in the same place and soothes himself with chimeric visions.

Other people distract themselves from unrewarding lives through movies, TV, alcohol and other mindless pastimes—anything to wipe reality from view. But to unleash your power, you have to remove the blinders, renounce the false dreams and distractions and confront reality head on.

The real world is where you must build your personal dream, and the real world is where you must fight to make that dream a reality. Resist the temptation to indulge in empty dreaming. Enact your dream in real life, with real people and real actions. Nurture your dream, yes, but not with childish fantasies. Apply your imagination and energy to the job of actualizing your dream in the real world.

You have to dream for anything to exist. Every product ever invented was first conceived in someone's mind. What is your vision? What do your senses tell you? How does your dream look, feel, sound, smell and taste? The dream is the experience. It is not the same as a goal. Goals are the quantifiable events leading to the dream. Ask yourself with uncompromising seriousness: what exactly do I desire most in life? Concentrate on envisioning exactly what you want and need.

People talk about buying dream houses, or landing dream jobs. These are legitimate dreams, but they are incomplete. Expand your dream beyond the fine house, the new car and the ideal job—beyond having a family and putting the children through college. Enlarge your dream to include the enrichment of your entire life and the legacy you will leave behind when it's over.

Imagine all the details, with everything the way you desire it. What sort of person are you? What do people say about you? In what ways do you contribute to society? Where do you live and with whom? How do you spend your days? How do the seasons unfold?

At age 50, Bill Gates, the world's richest and most celebrated entrepreneur, announced his intention to retire from his full-time role at Microsoft and shift his attention to heading the Bill and Melinda Gates Foundation, the world's largest philanthropic organization, which has donated billions of dollars to health and education projects, particularly in poor nations. Mr. Gates transformed the software industry and the computer industry, and his actions suggest that he will transform the humanitarian and charitable sectors as well.

Dare to dream expansively, beyond anything you've heretofore imagined. But don't stop there. Relentlessly pursue the dream by creating a life map that includes a series of goals designed to lead you to your ultimate destination. Then begin the journey.

Remember this ...

- Avoid false dreams and escapist fantasies.

- Dream large—then larger still.

- Actualize your dream in the real world, with real people and real effort.

- The journey to your dream begins with the first step.

Try this ...

Pick an idea, or a fragment of an idea, for a product you could invent, a business you could create, or an improvement you could make within your current job or company. Dozens of such ideas have probably crossed your mind. This time hold onto the idea for at least 30 minutes. Go to a quiet place, close your eyes and let the idea take shape. (If you start to fall asleep, open your eyes and focus on the sky or a pleasant landscape.) Furnish and cast the dream as you would a play, gradually filling in more and more detail. Direct the action to achieve the desired results, solving problems as they arise. When 30 minutes are up, write a summary of the dream, seal it in an envelope and file it away for at least one month. Then, if you judge it worthy of further development, devise a realistic plan with goals and a timeline.

10

Design a Life Map

"Order is not pressure which is imposed on society from without, but an equilibrium which is set up from within."
—*Jose Ortega y Gasset*

Your options in life are virtually unlimited. You can go in any direction you choose. In the large scheme of things, you can do anything you want to do. Circumstances that tend to pose limits, such as income, education or family issues, don't necessarily restrict you. The mere fact that you are reading this book tells me that you have advantages over 90 percent of the people on this earth. Don't be among those sad souls who, despite these many advantages, waste time comparing themselves with celebrities they see on TV.

You are not on this earth very long, so figure out where you want to go, what you want to accomplish and what responsibilities and obligations you are willing to assume.

Life is a highway with many possible routes. Each main route leads to branching routes, and every intersection has the potential to alter your direction. When you make a choice, some avenues are automatically cut off. To turn around and retrace your course is often impossible. When you start a family with one person, you end the possibility of having a family with someone else. When you accept one job, all other job offers disappear. When you move to the country, the excitement of urban living fades to memory.

When you elect to spend two hours of leisure time watching television, you pay a cost. To borrow a term from economics, the *opportunity cost* of your decision is equal to the total value of the other activities you could have pursued, but decided not to do, during those two hours. If you decided against taking a walk, or reading a book, or playing with your child, the benefits of those activities are the price you paid for the decision you made.

In *Through the Looking Glass*, Alice asks the Cheshire Cat which road she should take. When he inquires as to her destination, she claims ignorance. He replies, "If you don't know where you are going, any road will take you there." And with those words the Cheshire Cat becomes one of the most frequently quoted experts on time and life management in Western civilization.

If you don't know where you are going in life, one direction will do as well as another. If you are the kind of person who just lets life happen—a *reactive* rather than a *proactive* person—then it doesn't much matter what route you choose.

If, on the other hand, you have a dream of the life you want to lead, then make it a habit to always take the long view. Be aware of the consequences—the opportunity costs—of every decision. Know what you are giving up when you choose a particular course of action. When you enter one door, be aware that adjacent doors are closing. To the extent possible, figure out what lies behind each of those doors before you step through.

Create a mental map. Call it your life map, with your personal dream as the ultimate destination and specific interim points along the route. These interim points are your goals. Each one is a weigh station, a place to assess your progress, review your map and refuel for the next leg of the journey. Very few people can start off, follow a straight course, and arrive at their dream in one uninterrupted trip. Planning a succession of shorter-term goals is essential.

If you are a visual learner, or like to draw, create a physical map. Use a large sheet of sturdy paper. Cut photographs and illustrations from magazines to represent your dream and the goals along the way. Or draw them yourself using meaningful icons and symbols. Plot the main route, branching routes and side trips in pencil, or use string so that you can more easily plot course corrections.

Once you are on the road, enjoy the trip. The adventure of being alive is too precious to squander in the rush to reach your destination. If you can't cope with the speed and flow of the trip, slow it down. This is your journey and your map, so set reasonable speed limits. You are the driver.

Remember this ...

- Create a mental map to your dream—a plan.

- At each intersection, choose your direction carefully.

- Evaluate the "opportunity cost" of every decision you make.

- Control the speed and flow of the trip.

- Enjoy the journey.

Try this ...

Talk to people who seem to be living their dream. Ask them questions about how they got there. Find out how much they preconceived and how much they attribute to luck. Ask how they overcame doubts and where they found inspiration. If you can't find someone to interview, read biographies and autobiographies of successful people.

11

Set Challenging Interim Goals

"There are risks and costs to a program of action. But they are far less than the long-range risks and costs of comfortable inaction."
—*John F. Kennedy*

Life is like a path that forks and twists continually and usually without any warning whatsoever. You have a choice. You can meander through life without a plan, trying this fork or that. You can use all sorts of methods to make navigational decisions—how you feel at the moment, intuition, the flip of a coin, what other people think—or you can make a plan and determine your direction by consulting the plan.

Imagine two drivers departing from the same location at the same time, heading for the same destination. One uses a map, the other doesn't. The driver with the map travels straight to her destination, arriving in a reasonable period of time with few problems along the way. The driver without a map makes several wrong turns, gets lost, runs out of gas, goes miles out of his way and reaches the destination very late, if at all.

Goals are the milestones on the road to your dream. The dream is a relatively fixed point on your mental map. What you must do now is establish the interim points along the route that must be reached and passed on the way to this desired objective. A goal is an interim destination and the focus of intervening work. Goals are tactical. Many goals will have to be achieved to fully accomplish your dream.

What is the essential first step on your path to your dream? What is the second? Begin to lay out a plan and a tentative timeline. A logical and complete progression of goals can sometimes be foreseen in advance. For example, if your dream is to live with your family on a remote paradisiacal island while writing wildly popular best-selling novels, you may be able to project all of your educational, professional and personal goals with a fair amount of precision over a ten-year period.

On the other hand, defining the entire progression in advance may be impossible. Perhaps you can see only five years ahead, but sense that reaching your dream will take 20 years. That's okay. As you focus on existing goals, the remaining goals will take shape at the appropriate time. For example, you may be certain that you want to become a physician, but delay choosing a specialty until your last year of medical school.

When you are ready to set your first goal, make it specific and measurable. Describe the goal in as much detail as possible so that the target is clearly visible. If your goal is a house in the country, imagine how a lengthy real-estate listing might describe it—square footage, lot size, price, number of bedrooms and bathrooms and all the special features and bonuses in compelling detail.

Do not set impossible goals. Aim high, but be realistic in defining the nature of the goal and the time required to reach it. Pie-in-the-sky planning causes painful crashes.

Set goals in different areas of your life—professional, educational, recreational, emotional, spiritual and family. Goals don't have to be material. They can be creative, intellectual and philanthropic. If the consumption of goods is your only goal, boredom will soon sidetrack you. The worship of possessions, like a falling weight, anchors the senses and deadens the imagination, rendering you earthbound. Not that materialism is an inherent block to growth. Enjoyment of possessions in itself is healthy. Becoming obsessed with acquiring more and more things is not. Many insecure and fractured personalities acquire houses and storage rooms full of things, like layers of fat on the body. This weight of objects is often a misdirected attempt to build a sense of solidity, but ends up creating inertia. The worship of things is a great impediment to goal attainment. It is not money that is the root of all evil. Money is merely a very useful tool. It is the love of money that is hollow. A desperate need for material reassurance only creates conflict, insecurity, and failure of nerve.

Don't "borrow" goals from fellow travelers. Just because friends or coworkers have chosen a particular direction doesn't mean the same direction is right for you. Be secure enough to choose your own path. If you lack certainty, give it some time to develop. Gather more information about your choices and spend additional time examining your desires and motives.

Insecurity breeds conformity and conformity breeds apathy. Without a truly important set of goals, you will experience a gradual waning of will and the eventual death of purpose.

Looking inside yourself requires incredible courage, but holds boundless rewards. Knowing truly why you want something can eliminate worthless time-wasting goals. You should always strive to focus all your energy and life force upon the highest achievements that you can envision. But make sure they are the right ones for you.

Each challenge you meet and conquer will strengthen you for the next hill to climb. Get addicted to the feeling of success. Be greedy to experience the satisfaction of accomplishing what you set out to do. Enjoy the snowballing effect as your pace accelerates and gains force.

Remember this ...

- Goals are interim points on the path to your dream.

- Develop goals in different areas of your life.

- Material goals alone are not sufficient.

- Set challenging goals that are specific, measurable and realistic.

Try this ...

Set a goal in most major areas of your life: education, family, social, work/career, spiritual, health/fitness and community. Ask yourself how each of these goals will contribute to the attainment of your ultimate dream. Though the connection may be indirect, it is important to understand how all of your goals work in concert.

12

Continuously Evaluate Goals

"Imagination is the beginning of creation. You imagine what you desire, you will what you imagine, and at last you create what you will."
—*George Bernard Shaw*

You are far less likely to achieve ill-conceived goals than carefully chosen ones, so take time to verify that each new goal is the right one for you.

Maybe you are unsure whether you even have goals. Don't worry. If you got up this morning with an idea in mind of what you wanted to accomplish today, then you have goals. If you have a pretty good idea how you want to spend your vacation, when and where you hope to buy your first (or next) house, or what kind of car you plan to purchase when your current vehicle wears out, you have goals. They may not be precisely conceived and articulated, but they guide your thoughts and actions nonetheless. The question is, are they the right goals?

Most people set goals for other people's reasons. They choose the college that their parents favor, take the courses required by the system, look for jobs in the obvious places, and figure on building a life pretty much like their friends have, or their parents before them. Unless they've had exceptional career and personal guidance, they fail to consider even a small fraction of the possibilities, or whether their choices are the best ones for them. If you don't believe in what you are trying to accomplish, you will never reach your goals.

I want you to take one simple step right now. Its importance cannot be overstated, so concentrate. Rid your mind of distractions. This exercise may profoundly influence your direction for the remainder of your life.

Beginning where you presently are and working backwards, evaluate all previous goals. What goals (or decisions) led directly to your present job and income, family composition, living situation and state of health? What goals preceded those? Follow this reverse course as far as you can—back to the time in your life when you first identified your strongest interests, talents and abilities. If you diligently follow the progression of goals, you will see how each one built upon the one before, propelling you through a long series of steps to this moment.

Before you go to the next step, take some time to process what you learned about yourself by examining past goals. For example, have you tended to follow the path of least resistance? Do you typically look for opportunities, or wait for them to find you? How much did other people's opinions influence your previous goals? Are you trying to emulate, compete with, or surpass a particular person? Who?

Now evaluate your current goals. If you don't have them recorded, write them down. Be specific. If some of your goals are nebulous, try to make them solid. Define them exactly. Be honest and think carefully. Determine what you actually want and need from life.

Now look at the list and imagine how each goal will build upon the next like a series of steps leading to that ultimate achievement—your dream of the life you wish to lead. Answer these questions:

Which goals clearly create a path to your dream? Not every goal will be directly or indirectly linked to the life you ultimately envision. However, those that are should be given top priority in terms of time and energy. I'm not recommending that you drop unrelated goals, only that you be aware of their relative importance to the long-range picture.

How did each of these goals come to be important to you? Trace the genesis of each goal. Determine whether you became convinced of its importance independently or at the urging of someone else. Take a long, hard, honest look at any goals that were "lifted" intact from the life plan of a friend or influential person in your life.

What is your true motive for choosing each goal? Taking one goal at a time, ask yourself, "Why do I want this?" Write down your answer, read it back and ask, "Why is that important?" Again, record your answer, read it back and ask, "Why?" Keep asking why until you discover the fundamental underlying reason why you chose that goal. Your final answer may surprise you. You may realize that what you really want is something entirely different than you thought, and that you can achieve it in other, more appropriate ways.

For example, one of Jim's goals is to earn an advanced degree in business (an MBA). Jim asks himself, "Why do I want this?" His answer: to be qualified for advancement within his company. Then he asks himself, "Why is advancement important?" The answer: he wants to make more money. Why? To feel and appear successful. Why? To impress other people. Why? So they will admire and respect him.

Jim is seeking admiration and respect through one of the most conventional avenues known to man (and, increasingly, women): job status. Notice that he doesn't desire the MBA out of a love for business theory and practice. Nor does he want the MBA because he is committed to helping his company grow and succeed. Jim can probably win the admiration and respect of others in dozens of different ways. Maybe this isn't the best choice for Jim.

The goals you choose must be the correct goals to accomplish what you truly want to experience. It's one thing to aim for the right target and miss. It's quite another to set your sights on the wrong target in the first place.

To achieve personal power you must engage in an ongoing process of setting, evaluating and achieving goals that steadily move you toward your ultimate dream. As you acquire focus, your progress will accelerate.

Remember this ...

- Goal-setting is the ongoing process that propels you in the direction of your ultimate dream.

- Working backwards from the present, evaluate previous goals.

- Look at patterns in your goal-setting behavior.

- List your present goals in as much detail as possible.

- Evaluate each goal, where it came from and why it is important.

Try this ...

When you evaluate previous goals, include every major accomplishment, whether or not you consciously thought of it as a goal. For example, you may have mastered the violin because your parents expected you to, not because you chose the instrument yourself. That's important information. When you have a complete list going all the way back to childhood, pay particular attention to the goals you chose for yourself. These will tell you a great deal about the values you have carried into adulthood.

13

Resolve Inner Conflicts

"People grow through experience if they meet life honestly and courageously. This is how character is built."
—*Eleanor Roosevelt*

In the process of setting and pursuing your goals, you will discover many facets of your identity—your many selves, so to speak. Typically, some of them will turn out to be in conflict. For example, one part of you may be a home-loving person who desires a secure family life, while another part dreams of a fast life of fame and wealth. A third part of you may crave an existence devoted to learning or spiritual realization. These conflicts need to be resolved. No "maximum" can be reached when confusion fragments the whole.

Begin by isolating the values that anchor your goals. Try to understand exactly what motivates you. Values begin developing in childhood, so recall important experiences and lessons from your formative years. Many of your values were probably modeled or directly taught to you by your parents. Others may have been learned through religious instruction, scouting organizations, school and various activities.

Two kinds of values guide our lives: moral values and lifestyle values. Both influence goal selection. Moral values are the principles or standards by which we measure right and wrong decisions, good and bad conduct, desirable and undesirable behavior. Lifestyle values are strong preferences that determine with whom we associate, how and where we spend our time and other decisions that profoundly shape our lives. A love of music is a lifestyle value that motivates decisions related to education (music lessons), home design (state-of-the-art sound system), and leisure activities (concert attendance). A passion for surfing is a lifestyle value that is bound to influence where a person lives. If either kind of value directly conflicts with one or more goals, or if two goals based on opposing values conflict with each other, a head-on collision is practically inevitable.

None of your goals can be reached if you are not moving forward with unified resolve and complete conviction. Without unity, achieving your vision is like herding cats. So examine your goals and look for possible conflicts. Try to determine the source of any confusion you find.

Once you identify divisions, you must choose between them. This is a tough task, but an essential part of the journey. A common example is the man or woman who desires a family, but avoids commitment like a death sentence. The only socially acceptable way to remove this impasse is to choose one value over the other. Either get over the commitment fear or subtract family from the goal equation.

Another example is the would-be painter who cannot tolerate a disorderly environment of open tubes, paint smears, dirty brushes and unfinished canvases. If the need for a fastidious environment can't be mitigated, this person needs to develop a different career goal.

In choosing between values, stay close to the values you love most. Attempting to subjugate a great passion is not only tragic, it is usually a waste of time. Sooner or later the thing you love will reassert itself. On the other hand, if the thing you love resembles more an addiction than a value, do your best to overcome it. For example, it's entirely possible to love food and still become a fashion model. However, if the "love" is in reality an addiction to overeating the wrong kinds of foods, the problem is not a conflict of values but a destructive behavior.

Weigh conflicting values and goals carefully before deciding where and how much to prune. Invest in a thorough understanding of what you want, why you want it, and how it aligns with the other goals leading to your dream.

Remember this ...

- Identify and reconcile conflicting goals or desires.

- Define the values that anchor your goals.

- Moral values are measures of right and wrong.

- Lifestyle values define how you spend your time.

- Weigh conflicting values and goals carefully before deciding where and how much to prune.

Try this ...

Here are six universal moral values: truthfulness, respect, responsibility, kindness, fairness and citizenship. These values are taught (sometimes by different names) by all major religions of the world. What moral values would you include on your own personal list? Why? What does each mean to you and how will it influence your goals and life map?

14

Overcome Roadblocks

"Many of life's failures are people who did not realize how close they were to success when they gave up."
         —Thomas Edison

An important step to goal attainment that people often overlook is anticipating and clearing roadblocks. The best planning in the world won't get you to your goal if around the first turn you find the road washed out and have no alternative routes.

Roadblocks can be external factors over which you have little or no control, internal weaknesses over which you have a great deal of control (if you'll use it), and temporary setbacks caused by common emotional responses.

First, the external factors. The company for which you have worked for 10 years encounters severe legal problems and folds. You lose not only your job, health benefits and retirement, but the specific plan for career advancement crucial to achieving your dreams.

One way businesses deal with external forces is to develop contingency plans. It doesn't hurt to do that in your personal life. Prepare for unforeseen circumstances by having a fall-back position or an acceptable alternative. Think about how you might detour around roadblocks without upsetting your plans too much.

Internal weaknesses call for constant vigilance coupled with remedial efforts. One reason people don't accomplish their goals is because they don't have the courage to look at themselves, admit their shortcomings and start the painful process of change. It can be very difficult to recognize your own faults.

Just as repeatedly climbing to the top of a skyscraper can gradually reduce the fear of heights, confronting a situation you have long avoided can build confidence. What characteristics or habits are most likely to get in your way? Anger? Jealousy? Procrastination? Laziness? Dig deep into yourself and make an honest appraisal. See yourself clearly. Don't gloss over faults and shortcomings that you long ago accepted as inevitable.

On the other hand, don't try to become someone you are not. Being a naturally quiet person, for example, is not a fault. Neither is lacking a quick sense of humor or having a goofy smile. Accept the things you cannot readily control and concentrate on the traits, habits and behaviors that can be changed.

Which brings us to the third category of roadblocks: temporary setbacks caused by common emotional responses. I'm going to discuss four: 1) the slump that follows a major accomplishment, 2) comparing yourself to others, 3) lagging creativity, and 4) feeling that you don't deserve success. Look for one of these when your journey toward a goal becomes mysteriously stalled, you feel frustrated by the lack of progress and can't figure out what's wrong.

It's common to experience a lull after reaching a major goal. The problem may be due to something very simple, such as focusing on what you just accomplished instead of turning your attention to the next goal. If you don't know your next goal, get busy and set one.

A slump can also be born of the temporary slowdown that follows goal attainment. If you've been in high gear for a long time, relaxing may be difficult. Like the runner who feels lethargic and guilty if she stops her training routine for even a few days, you start to blame yourself for being in neutral. Don't. Give yourself permission to rest and regenerate.

Finally, don't compound the situation with worry. If you start thinking you've "lost it" and become panicky, fear itself can quickly create a self-fulfilling prophesy.

Comparing yourself to others is a common problem that produces all sorts of bad feelings, including the urge to give up. You can always find people who have "more" of something than you do—more sales, more charisma, more income, more leadership ability, more knowledge, more eloquence, more beauty. However, repeatedly feeding yourself poor evaluations based on negative comparisons only leads to depression and further decline. Instead, maximize your strengths and concentrate on becoming the most effective person you can possibly be.

Sometimes a great deal of creativity is required to reach a goal. The usual approaches simply don't work. Try to look at the challenge from a different perspective. Hold a brainstorming session with one or more clever friends or coworkers. Do something physical that doesn't require much thought, allowing your subconscious mind to produce new ideas in the process. Read the biographies of creative people. Meditate for 15 minutes before planning sessions and play Mozart in the background while you work.

I've known highly talented, determined people who back off just when a goal at long last comes into view. As far as I can determine, these people believe deep inside that they don't deserve to be rewarded, and experience guilt and despair at the prospect of success. To feel better, they must fail, so at the last minute they resort to self-sabotage. They go on an alcoholic binge, fail to show up at a crucial meeting, have an extramarital affair, or "get caught" in some other self-defeating behavior. Often they have no notion of the real motive behind their failure. Admittedly, these are extreme examples. The disturbing thing is that many less self-destructive people seem to have a touch of the same affliction. Maybe they're afraid of the additional responsibilities that accompany success, or don't think they can maintain the higher level of prosperity. Change, particularly rapid change, can be very difficult to manage.

If you sense a fear of success within yourself, begin preparing for the transition now. Read some materials on change and, if necessary, seek professional counseling. Each time you bravely delve into the core issues that provoke insecurity and doubt, you come closer to realizing your dream.

Remember this ...

- Develop contingency plans for overcoming roadblocks.
- Identify and control traits and tendencies that may get in your way.
- When you reach a goal, give yourself permission to rest and regenerate. Then set a new goal.
- Don't compare your progress to that of others.
- Learn to manage the difficult transitions that sometimes accompany change.

Try this ...

When you set a new goal, list possible roadblocks in advance. Obviously you can't foresee all of them, but some will be relatively predictable. For example, a potential roadblock to completing college is depleting your college fund before you finish. Anticipating roadblocks and inventing ways around them can be a very beneficial step in the goal-setting process.

15

Pledge Total Commitment

"If I fail, it will be for lack of ability, and not of purpose."
—*Abraham Lincoln*

To strive or not to strive. That is the commitment question. Any attempt to achieve a challenging goal produces stress. The more challenging the goal, the greater the stress.

Those inner screams of mental pain and emotional fear that often accompany stress greatly intensify the urge to let go. It's not unusual to become confused, to think, "Just give it up—forget about it. It's too hard. You were a fool to try it in the first place. Take the loss. You should have known you couldn't do it, you loser."

Often the voices of discouragement include those of friends and loved ones. Some hate seeing you suffer. Others fear you might succeed and make them look like failures by comparison.

In the darkest hours of World War II, as Germany seemed certain to invade England and destroy his beloved homeland, Prime Minister Winston Churchill spoke to his people of courage. He told them that to quit was spiritual suicide. In his office, Churchill posted a sign like the one on the following page.

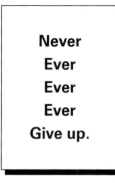

**Never
Ever
Ever
Ever
Give up.**

At times of low energy and high stress, you will tend to falter. Whether the problem is low finances, a personal breakup, poor health, or failed goals, your doubts will feed a growing urge to let go. Quitting will seem like the wisest, least painful option.

This powerful urge to accept defeat is not merely the rational mind rebelling, the emotional mind gets into the act as well. Quitting can be a form of self-punishment for not achieving. If you have chronically low self-esteem, quitting allows you to kick yourself for years over another lost opportunity.

How can you mitigate the tendency to weaken and fail in your commitment? Sometimes the crisis is in the body itself.

Lance Armstrong, an American hero in the eyes of many, defeated almost certain death from cancer and returned to professional cycling to become the most decorated Tour de France winner in history. Few people realize that Armstrong attributes his repeated victories in part to the cancer, which taught him to accept pain.

A great rider must surrender to suffering during the brutal mountain-climbing stages of the Tour de France. According to Armstrong, those climbs made him laugh. The pain of pushing mile after mile up grueling grades was a joke compared to the agonies he experienced throughout his battle with cancer. Instead of destroying him, cancer taught him how to win. In a sense, it became his strongest ally.

Before his life-and-death trial by cancer, Armstrong was a mediocre climber by world standards. Most athletes in his position would have quit. While he lay in his hospital bed feeling old and weak and sick, as if he were indeed already dying, his team manager came in, said a few words of consolation and informed Armstrong that the team no longer needed him—he was fired.

Think of the worst tragedy that could possibly come your way. Ironically, that tragedy could awaken strengths you never knew you had. For a year or more, Lance Armstrong's future was in doubt. No one thought he would race again. Yet, after studying at the feet of that terrible mentor, cancer, Armstrong knew he could reach a level of striving beyond any previously measured. When he raced again, his old comrade, pain, discouraged his competitors while Armstrong briskly climbed away. Now the others raced for second place.

The mind is like a fist. Once clenched upon an object, a fist must exert energy in order to sustain a concentrated grip. The longer the object is grasped, the harder it is to allot the required energy. The fingers tire. The arm and shoulder ache. But at the same time, the sustained effort causes the arm to strengthen, and the longer the fist holds on, the easier it becomes.

Remember this image when your mind aches from striving and you want desperately to relax your efforts. It will get easier as you get stronger. Don't let go.

Remember this ...

• Like Winston Churchill, never, ever, ever give up.

• Like Lance Armstrong, laugh in the face of pain.

• The longer you hold on, the easier it will become.

Try this ...

Recall the last time you gave up on a goal, or failed to finish a project. Maybe you decided to study the piano, but quit after only a few lessons. Or perhaps you tried to change your eating habits, but quickly succumbed to cravings for sweets and fast food. Try to remember the moment when your commitment failed. How did you feel? What sensations and emotions were you experiencing? Now imagine yourself holding on for just one more hour or one more day. See yourself moving past that critical point when giving up seemed like the only option. Rehearse the scene over and over in your mind. Then, the next time your commitment falters, be ready. Don't let go.

16

Become a Fortress

"I know how men in exile feed on dreams of hope."
—Aeschylus

Until you have created an internal unity of resources, you cannot steadily and consistently move toward your goals. Until your walls are strong, you can neither protect yourself, nor anyone else. Unless your powers are united, you are weak. What is the answer? How best can you unite your divided resources? How best can you shelter those you love? Become a fortress.

A fortress is a stronghold with solid walls that shield it from outside forces. It is situated to provide protection and good visibility for defense purposes. Inside is a bustling community in which everything and everyone is organized for maximum strength and efficiency. Visitors approaching the fortress are spotted while still miles away, in plenty of time to determine whether they are friends or enemies. Peaceful emissaries and traders are welcomed through the fortress gates. Known and potential enemies are turned away. A well designed and equipped fortress thrives on a combination of self-sufficiency and judicial openness.

Having strong "walls" means that you have a secure sense of yourself as an individual. You keep your own counsel and are not unduly influenced by others. Having good "visibility" means that you are a keen observer of everything around you, able to readily identify and assess events in your environment. You harbor a "bustling community" of inner resources—intelligence, talents, skills, emotional awareness, physical strength and agility, and spiritual certainty—that operates with precision and harmony. You are growing and expanding, but on your own terms.

Please don't misunderstand. The fortress I envision is not closed to, or in any way isolated from, the rest of the world. On the contrary, it's an active trading center, where information and ideas are exchanged and talents and resources are shared.

I have met people who give the impression of being impenetrable. Nothing seems to hurt them, but nothing touches them either. Trying to have meaningful dialogue on most topics is fruitless because these individuals already hold rigid opinions and positions on almost every topic. No independent thinker will attempt to collaborate long with such people.

In contrast, to become a fortress of one, you must develop integrity. That's right, plain old-fashioned integrity. Integrity, after all, is really about wholeness—a unity of beliefs, words and actions. People of integrity are complete and undivided. They do not go around saying one thing while doing another. They don't loudly claim a particular faith or ideology and then live in daily defiance of its tenets. They don't make promises that they have no intention of keeping, or agree to a plan of action just to appease the other person. Integrity is the fortress I'm talking about.

Inside the strong, protective walls of this kind of fortress, the people you love—children, parents, spouse, partner, friends, associates—will thrive with you and learn to mirror your integrity.

Start building your fortress now. The first step is to make the decision to change. Find out where you are deficient and fill the gaps. Assess your inner resources and bring them into alignment. If some habit (indecision, procrastination, heavy drinking, overeating, TV) is sabotaging your effectiveness, do something about it. Hire professional help, if necessary, to get to the bottom of it and root it out.

Pay particular attention to fear. Fear is at the bottom of many destructive behaviors and debilitating habits. Fear of failure, fear of commitment, fear of pain, fear of abandonment, fear of success—any of these can blast a hole as big as Texas in your fortress walls. Fear can decay the strongest citadel and cause its fall.

Remember this ...

- Become a fortress.

- Develop a secure sense of yourself as an individual.

- Be a keen observer of everything around you.

- Cultivate essential inner resources.

- Develop integrity—a unity of beliefs, words and actions.

- Identify and banish fear.

Try this ...

Decide who and what you want to include in your mental, emotional and spiritual "fortress." Which people will be protected within its walls? What rich harvest of ideas will be traded in its marketplace? How will its resources be renewed and how will you protect its boundaries? Create a mental image of your fortress. Carry it with you and feel its strength daily.

17

Defeat Inertia

"Experience is not what happens to a man; it is what a man does with what happens to him."

—Aldous Huxley

Countless people are stuck performing unproductive, unfulfilling routines. They are convinced that life is destined to produce more of the same, because they never break the pattern long enough to recognize the alternatives. Besides, a humdrum existence doesn't hurt as much when you refuse to recognize there is something better.

Many people feel they have no choice but to keep doing whatever has worked in the past, regardless of its limitations. Like windup dolls, they get up each day and eat the same breakfast, drive the same route to work, do their assigned job in the prescribed way, go home at the appointed hour, have dinner and watch TV until they get sleepy and set their bedside alarms to arise and repeat the same pattern the following day.

Many of the excuses people give for not enlarging the narrow orbits that govern their lives really add up to something called inertia—resistance to change. Borrowed from physics, the term refers to an object's tendency to keep doing whatever it is presently doing. If it is still, it remains still. If it is moving, it keeps moving in the same direction. Inertia is what locks people into repetitious routines day after day, week after week, year after year. Inertia is what gets people stuck in dead-end jobs and destructive relationships.

To overcome inertia you have to apply force. A force will make something that is still start to move, like kicking a soccer ball with your foot will make the ball roll. To move a person off dead center might require the force of a personal crisis, or a natural disaster. We've all heard stories about the sedentary person who suffered a heart attack, begrudgingly started to exercise and eventually became a marathon runner. The lives of thousands of people are regularly shattered by hurricanes and earthquakes. In just a few seconds, every ritual and routine, regardless of its value, is disrupted—sometimes forever.

To slow or stop something (or someone) that is already in motion requires the force of resistance. The rolling soccer ball will be slowed or stopped by the resistance of the turf over which it passes. People are forced to curtail or abandon established routines by things like illness, being fired and winning the lottery.

If you are experiencing inertia, start looking for ways to force change. I'm not advocating that you engineer a personal crisis, an illness, or a natural disaster, but find some means of interrupting the sameness and monotony that govern your life. Don't let yourself become so exhausted or complacent that you have no wish to look at the outside world. Break the routine of the day for just a few moments. This will give you hope. This will create awareness and the will to take additional, longer breaks.

Inform yourself about the endless possibilities that exist in life. Read news stories and biographies. Every week, visit a place in your community that you have never before been to—a business, museum, gallery, construction site, lecture, or university campus. Talk to the people you see there.

You must know of the existence of an alternative before you can choose it. You must recognize that a different life is possible, that it is more than a fantasy. Some people know, but don't think they are smart enough. Others are reticent and wait to be "discovered." Still others are afraid of failure—or success. Whatever is immobilizing you, reject it and get moving.

You have been given a limited time on earth. You have been issued a body, a mind and unique talents, and have a powerful obligation to develop them. Don't allow your potential to lie fallow and neglected. If left latent long enough, it will wither and fade away. No waste is more tragic.

You have the power to defeat inertia. Start now—forcefully.

Remember this ...

- Inertia can keep you stuck in unproductive routines, a dead-end job or a destructive relationship.

- To overcome inertia, force one small change—then another.

- Think of ways to interrupt sameness, monotony and mechanical routines.

- Find the edge of your "comfort zone" and step beyond it. Try new activities. Visit unfamiliar places.

Try this ...

Just for the stimulation of it, change one routine every week. Take a different route or mode of transportation to work. Replace the morning paper with a book of poetry. Try a different form of exercise. Change the way you approach problems and decisions. If you usually attack them in isolation, call up a trusted friend or colleague and begin the process instead with a lively discussion. Defeat inertia with a succession of small changes.

18

Project Vitality

"There is a vitality, a life force, an energy, a quickening, that is translated through you into action, and because there is only one of you in all time, this expression is unique. And if you block it, it will never exist through any other medium and will be lost."
—*Martha Graham*

Vitality is the capacity to live, grow and develop. It's the characteristic or force that distinguishes living things from non-living things. You were born with vitality, and if you are reading these words, you still have it. Vitality is your most powerful asset, your prime resource in life. If you have squandered your vitality over the years, it's time to get it back.

Think of the most vigorous, enthusiastic, energetic person you know. Where does that person's vitality come from? Good genes? While genetics may play a role, there's little evidence that energy and its opposite, lethargy, are inherited traits. Luck? I've had total strangers say to me, "You're so lucky to be thin." I hasten to tell them that luck has nothing to do with it. I'm convinced luck plays no role in producing spirit and hustle either.

Here's another thing I'm sure of: cheating never works. The hyper, jittery brand of energy produced by caffeine and stimulant drugs is no substitute for true vitality. In fact, drugs cheat vitality the same way plagiarizing cheats your brain—by depriving you of development. Furthermore, reliance on drugs demands a huge payback and, like most gambling, the odds are with the house.

In Goethe's *Faust*, the all-knowing Mephisto informs Faust that the only means to a long, healthy life is a rudimentary lifestyle—basic food in moderation, daily physical work and deep sleep at night. Nourishment, exercise and sleep combined with a positive attitude—these are healthy sources of vitality.

You know better than anyone if your diet needs improving. You can rationalize the donuts, hamburgers and soft drinks all you want, if your daily allotment of calories is being squandered on sugary, high-fat foods, your body simply is not getting the nutrients it needs to build and maintain vitality. Weight is not the only issue, though vitality is difficult to sustain while carrying around twenty or more pounds of excess fat. Get your head out of the sand and your hand out of the cookie jar. Read up on the research and change your eating habits accordingly. Get addicted to fruits, vegetables, whole grain products and seafood. It can be done.

If climbing a flight of stairs or walking across a parking lot leaves you feeling exhausted, how can you possibly project vitality? You need exercise to build cardiovascular and muscle fitness. Muscle (including the heart muscle) is the engine of the body and needs to be kept in top operating condition. One of the reasons fitness programs often fail is that people want exercise to be easy. They don't persist long enough to develop the muscle mass needed for vigorous movement to feel natural and pleasurable. Vitality is not easily won.

Many people start working out in order to firm their bodies and look better, which entails eliminating excess fat and developing lean, sleek, shapely muscle. However, some people, especially women, worry that their muscles will get too big. That almost never happens. The vast majority of people don't have the right genetics to get excessively muscular, even if they want to. Build productive lean muscle tissue, which increases the basic metabolism, burning extra calories even while you rest. Adding and keeping just three new pounds of muscle can burn up to an additional 9,000 calories every month. Not only does the extra muscle help burn fat and calories, it takes up to 20 percent less space than fat. So a fit 140-pound person can wear clothes several sizes smaller that a fat 140 pound person. And lean muscle adds tone, shape, and firmness to your body.

Millions of people take drugs to get a decent night's rest. Direct marketing of prescription sleeping pills via television has reached staggering proportions, and I suspect many people are taking these drugs needlessly. Depending on which reports you read, sleep experts recommend between seven and nine hours of sleep to accomplish all the repairs, regeneration, rewiring and—yes—revitalization that your brain and body need. Eat right, exercise daily, get the TV out of your bedroom, and resolve any other issues that may be interfering with your ability to sleep. You can't be chronically sleep deprived and expect to achieve your maximum capabilities.

Mental vitality comes from being fully engaged, from giving complete attention and energy to the activity at hand, whether it's writing a computer program, painting a fence, or having a conversation with a friend. If you love what you are doing, all-out engagement comes easily. When your enthusiasm is less than robust, try loving the process itself—the satisfaction that comes from being alert, unselfconscious and totally absorbed in the present moment.

You have the means to project vitality in abundance, tempered, of course, by your personal style. Whether it's bubbling vivacity, charismatic authority, or glowing serenity, vitality is your birthright.

Remember this ...

- Vitality is born of the basics: wholesome food, vigorous exercise and adequate rest.

- Caffeine and stimulant drugs are no substitute for true vitality.

- To increase physical vitality, build muscle—the engine of the body.

- To maximize mental and emotional vitality, be fully engaged in the activity at hand.

Try this ...

Read some of the works of Mihaly Csikszentmihalyi, a psychologist who has studied and written about the concept of "flow." Flow is a unique state of concentration in which action seems to be effortless. In a state of flow, you perform at your peak and stretch beyond former limits. Emotions are positive and energized, yet your attention is so focused on the task at hand that you may not be aware of feelings at all except in retrospect. Everything but the task is forgotten — time, surroundings, even yourself. Csikszentmihalyi compares flow to what sports psychologists call reaching the "zone," a state of transcendent absorption that seems to push champion athletes beyond former limits.

19

Rid Yourself of Uncertainty

"Uncertainty is the very condition to impel man to unfold his powers."
—*Erich Fromm*

To be uncertain is to lack sure knowledge. An uncertain outcome is undetermined. An uncertain motive is questionable. An uncertain mind is undecided.

The whole point of learning is to build certainty. When you take a test, if you are uncertain of an answer you either guess or skip the question. When you are uncertain what product to buy, you read labels and consult experts. Scientists test hypotheses, doctors order lab work, economists analyze markets and mechanics tear apart motors—all in an effort to dispel uncertainty.

The whole point of decision-making is to resolve uncertainty. First you define the decision to be made. For simplicity's sake, let's say you need to decide what kind of car to buy. You are uncertain because you have choices. (If you lived on a remote island with only one available car and no access to more, the only uncertainty would be whether to drive at all.) So the first step is to gather information about such variables as price, features, gas mileage, safety and available financing. You evaluate the information and decide on, say, four alternatives. You then test-drive each one, which gives you additional information and allows you to narrow the field to two. Do you flip a coin to make the final decision? Probably not. Chances are you talk to acquaintances who own both types of cars, take more test-drives, discuss the options with your family and sleep on it. With each additional piece of information, uncertainty diminishes until finally you make your purchase.

Let's look at other uncertainties. What do you do if your job situation becomes uncertain? The company is laying off people and you start to feel insecure. Do you hunker down and try to become invisible? That may have worked in elementary school when you didn't know the answer to a question, but it won't work to preserve your job. One thing you can do is ask questions about the plan that is driving the layoffs. Someone might be able to tell you if and when your department is slated to become a target. Another thing you can do is work very hard to become the most valuable, adaptable, specialized employee in the company. And a third thing you can do is update your resume and start making inquiries at other companies. All three of these courses of action involve information and/or learning.

The most powerful approach to reducing uncertainty regarding your own performance is to prepare thoroughly. A public speaker writes and rewrites his speech, rehearses its presentation and timing, has all his visual aids organized and ready, arrives on time, checks all the equipment and delivers like a pro. If he experiences any stage fright at all, it is minimal.

Being uncertain what you stand for, or believe in, poses a more difficult problem. That kind of certainty requires self-knowledge—an understanding of your values and the principles that guide your life. Socrates was fond of saying that knowledge is the one and only good, while the ultimate evil is ignorance. Aristotle's view was harsher—that people of awareness were the living, and the unaware were the walking dead.

Self-knowledge builds self-confidence and centeredness. Without these anchoring forces, you are bound to drift. Where the current pulls, you follow. Without a center you are rudderless, blind, and lost at sea. Uncertainty is then your only certainty.

Most of us face ethical dilemmas and questions of morality almost daily. If you lack the moral code or spiritual compass to fix your position with certainty, this is the area of self-knowledge you should work on first and with greatest diligence. You cannot depend on yourself to make right decisions if you lack the means to evaluate information and alternatives in the first place.

Those who hope for the best while deferring decisions to others drift like lobotomized sheep into moral and intellectual death. "Do not go gently into the good night," wrote Dylan Thomas, as he fought against the forces of self-destruction eating away at him. Thomas knew that his personal demons never rested. And his great poetry never yielded to the dark side. Today we remember him for that courage.

Uncertainty, if yielded to, is the enemy of achievement. And yet uncertainty is always present. Deal with it through self-knowledge, learning and action. These three in combination ultimately erase uncertainty.

Remember this ...

- Build certainty through self-knowledge, learning and action.

- Use a sound decision-making process to resolve uncertainty.

- Remove uncertainty from any performance by being thoroughly prepared.

Try this ...

Look for signs of uncertainty related to each of your goals. Ask yourself what will reconcile or dispel any uncertainties you discover. Do you need to clarify your values (self-knowledge)? Do you need to gather additional facts or data (learning), or do you need to take some sort of action to jump-start your resolve?

20

Convert Doubt to Courage

"Doubt is thought's despair."
—*Kierkegaard*

Doubt is the absence of conviction. It is an attitude of skepticism and provisional disbelief. A skeptical person will demand to see compelling evidence before believing a claim or an allegation. Doubt is a function of the reasoning brain. It is highly valuable during planning, when careful deliberation maximizes good decision making.

Sometimes doubt serves as a caution against rash impulsivity. It can help avert a crisis by warning us when we might be in danger. For example, without a healthy skepticism, we would be easy prey for thousands of disreputable individuals and organizations selling bogus products and ideas through the Internet.

On the other hand, doubt, particularly self-doubt, can weaken resolve and become a dangerous mental habit. It can creep into every facet of our lives and increasingly infect our thinking. When that happens, doubt is a serious weakness that slows us down and, in the delay, invites disaster.

The decisive person learns when to use doubt and when to put it away. Doubt is a great enemy of action. Once you have decided upon a goal, set doubt aside. The time to doubt the wisdom of flying is before the plane takes off, not afterwards.

Decisions call for resolve, and yet self-doubt often persists. Many times, as you begin a difficult task, apprehension will taunt you and tempt you to change the plan. Misgivings will urge you to lower your expectations and lessen your goals. Insecurity will push you to reduce your invested time and energy, to turn down a different path or completely change directions. These are all manifestations of fear, their negative energy like a gun pointed at your own head.

Try not to doubt yourself, even if others do. Keep moving toward your goals. Regular evaluation of your progress will indicate if and when you need to adjust course. Don't do it based on irrational fears, and never give in to the naysayers.

Doubt is a human trait experienced by every explorer since time began. Yet history more often salutes those who courageously persist in the face of doubt than those who succumb and retreat. Nicholas Copernicus was one of the most courageous.

Many centuries ago, the earth was proclaimed by the Christian church to be the sacred celestial center of the entire universe—fixed and unmoving. The year was 1530, a century before the invention of even the crudest telescope. Copernicus, a church canon who practiced both medicine and astronomy, lifted his eyes to the sky and found inspiration in his ability to perceive.

One of his first discoveries was a crater on the moon. Diamond bright, its radiance shimmered in the shadows of the northwest quadrant. Copernicus gazed longingly at this rare and luminous beauty. He realized that the spot he saw was a crater, a relatively young and isolated hexagonal formation. Today the crater is named Copernicus in celebration of its namesake's courage.

In 1543, near his death, Copernicus published *De Revolutionibus*, which asserted that the earth rotated on its axis once daily and orbited around the sun once yearly. The ensuing scandal was immense. By openly refuting the official position of the church, Copernicus risked excommunication, torture and death as a heretic.

Copernicus traveled not by ship or horseback, but in the far superior vehicle of his mind, where doubt played a dual role. Keen powers of observation and deduction led him to doubt the teachings of the church, and the courage of his convictions helped him overcome self-doubt to become the father of modern astronomy.

Like Copernicus and other great explorers, you can transform doubt into a quiet, defiant resolve. Begin by identifying the source of doubt. Does it come to assist or to deny? Does it derive from a rational evaluation of the evidence, or from feelings of inferiority and unworthiness? If it is legitimate, you will actually improve your prospects for success by resolving the doubt. If it is illegitimate, courageously push doubt aside and press on.

Remember this...

- Learn when to use doubt and when to put it away.

- Once you have decided upon a goal, set doubt aside.

- When doubt surges, identify its source.

- Don't change course based on self-doubt or irrational fears.

Try this ...

A common source of self-doubt is comparing yourself to others. When a colleague gets a big commission check, or when someone with less seniority receives a plum project, you think, "What's wrong with me?" When self-doubts like this arise, take 10 minutes to refute them with specific, written affirmations. For example, write, "I'm no different from Sam. I too make big sales and get big commission checks," or "It's not true that Ann is better liked by the brass than I am. They have good reasons for their decisions. It's no reflection on me or my work." Keep writing for the full 10 minutes or until you feel your self-doubt begin to ebb, whichever comes first.

21

Reject the Idea of Failure

"Defeat doesn't finish a man—quitting does. A man is not finished when he is defeated. He's finished when he quits."
　　　　　　　　　　　　　　　　　—Richard M. Nixon

Run the best race you can run. When the contest is over, regardless of who wins, assess the results honestly. Did you play better this week than last? Did you apply all appropriate knowledge and skills? Did you train well? Did you put 100 percent effort into your performance? If you can answer yes to these questions, you are a winner, whether you take the prize or not. Punishing yourself for not being the best is a very harsh way to live your life.

Unless you believe you have failed, you have not. The very concept of failure is small-minded—the evil twin of self-defeat. It denies the capacity of people to learn from mistakes, to accrue mastery through methodical, measured improvement. Never say, "I am a failure." Merely giving breath to such treacherous, self-hating words is a betrayal. Furthermore, such statements can disastrously weaken your spirit.

Like a scientist, learn to view each failed attempt as trial and error, replete with vital information. Without failures, you cannot fine-tune your efforts. Failures are stepping stones to success, but only if you learn from them. Never despair. Every time you fall short of a goal, determine why. Analyze the experience to distill the vital information that will prevent the same error from occurring on your next try. Thomas Edison "failed" thousands of times in his quest to develop the incandescent light bulb, testing numerous materials in the filament before settling on carbon. When asked about his failures, he famously said, "I have not failed. I've just found 10,000 ways that won't work."

Fasten your mind around this concept: failure, until proven, is a fallacy. What constitutes proof? Total lack of success, which can't be measured until you abandon all effort. Therefore the only time you've failed is when you quit.

Occasionally someone tells me he has an "inferiority complex," or laments, "I can't win. I've never won anything in my life." Such statements are a loser's safety blanket. And like most safety blankets, eventually they become straightjackets. They provide the illusion of solace to people who view themselves as incapable. Failure is a comfort zone for defeatists who indulge in self-loathing and self-pity. Failure is safe because it is the bottom. The fall is over, you can't sink lower. Acceptance of failure is therefore either cowardice or a kind of mental illness. It violates all of our survival instincts and faith in life itself.

Practice patience. Give yourself time. Restless impatience to achieve a goal sometimes induces people to pronounce their efforts failed long before any such conclusions are warranted. Take time to finish each task. Acknowledge beforehand that adjustments will be necessary along the way. Be open to critical self-evaluation, but avoid making hasty judgments. Life in pursuit of a dream is lived on the border between success and failure. It is an exciting place to be. If you step across the line into failure, you will know soon enough and can adjust your course. You will learn from the experience and you will calculate your next step more precisely.

Be your own best friend—your most loyal comrade. Wipe your emotional and spiritual slate clean and begin fresh. Forgive yourself for past failings. Dig out the seeds of self-mistrust and self-loathing. Turn the page, learn and evolve. Recognize that both failure and success are self-defined. You are neither a failure nor a success until you believe that you are. Life is very large. Be large with it.

Remember this ...

• Failures are stepping stones to success.

• Self-evaluate, but don't make hasty judgments.

• The only true failure is in quitting.

• If you've done your best, you are a winner.

Try this ...

Think back to a recent experience in which your performance fell short of expectations—yours or someone else's. Evaluate the experience as objectively as you possibly can. Consider everything about the incident—its content, its effect on relationships, and any residual feelings you have (regret, resentment, embarrassment, etc.). Finally, list the lessons you learned from all aspects of the incident. A lesson in this context is an observation or insight that gives you beneficial new knowledge or wisdom that you can apply to future decisions.

22

Clarify Your Motives

When news breaks of a heinous crime, one of the first things we listen for is the motive. What caused the suspect to do it? we automatically wonder. The importance of motivation in explaining unlawful or tragic events is something we intuitively grasp, yet we rarely wonder what motivates honorable acts and great accomplishments. Nor do we question our own motives nearly as often as we should.

What is the deepest underlying motive driving each of your goals? Can you define it? Knowing the truth about why you want something can eliminate a worthless time-wasting goal and allow you to focus on higher achievements. If your goal to become a principal is motivated by a desire to escape classroom teaching, you might be better off switching fields, or resolving the issues that make your classroom such a disagreeable place to be. If your goal of having a lavish wedding is motivated by a desire to outdo the weddings of all your friends, perhaps the money should be invested elsewhere.

Defining your true motives requires honesty. Do you dare question why you want what you want, or why you fear what you fear? Deceiving yourself and others by pretending to have ambitious, high-minded motives when the truth is far less altruistic generally doesn't work. If your true motivation isn't strong enough to power your journey when the going is rough, you will never reach your goal.

Sometimes by digging deep, you will find that your true motive is not your own, but borrowed from a friend, or imposed upon you by a parent, spouse, employer or TV personality touting the benefits of a particular course of action. Countless millions, nagged by people close to them, attempt to stop smoking. Most say they want to quit, but fail. Why? Because the motivation is not their own. They do not have a true desire to change. A few rare individuals easily succeed, because the source of their motivation is internal. It is just that simple—they decided.

Sadly, the decisions of a great many people are controlled by the mass media. Such people are groping though life, conforming to the herd instinct. They no more know what they truly want than they know who they really are.

Like all humans, you respond to the law of universal gravitation and attraction—you exist in the force-field of others. But those "others" exist within your field of influence as well. Either they orbit around you, or you orbit around them. Many things determine who has the greater pull in interpersonal relationships. Reputation is a factor, along with social skills, knowledge, position power and tradition, among other things. However, when you know what you truly desire to have and become, you cease to perform as a kind of windup toy programmed by family, friends and society.

Choose goals that are genuinely important to you. Goals you believe in are intrinsically motivating. The incentives are built-in. Besides whatever tangible rewards they offer, their attainment delivers a sense of pride, satisfaction and heightened self-esteem. Other intangible incentives that serve as powerful motivators are personal growth, love, recognition and approval. When evaluating a possible goal, ask yourself if its realization will bring any of these rewards.

When a goal is necessary without being particularly inspiring (we can't avoid them), use extrinsic incentives to motivate yourself. Promise yourself a weekend getaway, dinner out, or a new outfit. For example, a necessary goal on your journey to an advanced degree might be to pass a dreaded statistics class. It may be tough to make yourself love that goal, but you can plan with your classmates to throw a big party when it's over. Celebration can be a reward in itself.

Another way to create motivation is to link goals to your personal code of conduct. For example, if your personal code specifies that you always keep your commitments, you will do whatever it takes to achieve a disagreeable goal just to avoid disappointing yourself.

Knowing your motives requires questioning events, ideas, desires and behavior with a dogged and relentless honesty. This is a continuous process and one that is mandatory to maximizing yourself and your achievements.

Remember this ...

• Question the motive behind every goal.

• Never concoct high-minded rationalizations to justify baser goals. Be honest.

• Avoid goals imposed by, or borrowed from, others.

• Choose intrinsically motivating goals—ones you believe in.

Try this ...

When you choose a new goal, take a few minutes to ask yourself, "Why do I want this?" Keep asking Why? until you discover the most basic underlying desire motivating you. Keep, discard or modify the goal accordingly.

23

Shape Up for Success

"The mind's first step to self-awareness must be through the body."
—*George Sheehan*

Maybe you think you look just fine. You've gained thirty pounds, but have excuses for the extra weight. Long hours at the desk. A touch of arthritis in the knees. You defend yourself with denial and wear loose garments. You cover the double chin with a beard and purchase dark clothing. You can no longer wear the well-cut clothes you once enjoyed and it depresses you just to think about it. You don't dare look as you pass the mirror after a shower or bath.

It's high-time to reject all this false witnessing. Regard yourself truthfully, starting with your body. I don't mean to sound like a fire-and-brimstone preacher, but there is no better way to begin your journey to self-empowerment than by dominating your flesh. There is no better, faster way to hone the force of your will.

Your body is the vehicle in which you travel through life. You have been issued one vehicle. It is the only one you will ever own and can never be replaced. What condition is it in? Is it shaking, smoking, twitching, slowing? Knowing the many miles this vehicle will have to cover, it's pretty foolish to ignore the maintenance requirements. It's senseless to spend money on paint jobs and polish while neglecting the fundamentals that keep it in good running condition.

The state of your body is a big, blinking neon sign of attitude and integrity. It is a program guide to your mental and physical health and vigor. Anyone can read it. Everyone does. The lazy, passive soul sinks into deeper and deeper levels of sloth and decay—premature death-acceptance—while the body evidences the decline. Oversize shirts and trousers don't hide anything.

Begin with a self-assessment. Don't be afraid. Try to work your way through this exercise without balking. Face yourself honestly. Like any other disagreeable task, this one requires courage. The first look is always the hardest.

Find a private place—a bedroom or bathroom with a full-length mirror. Enter and close the door. You want total privacy for this. Now, remove your clothes. All of your clothes. Stand before the mirror so that you can see your entire body. Forcing yourself to be calm, look at your body as though examining a foreign object. Look hard at what you see. Be brave and don't pretend it's better or worse than it is.

Shake yourself vigorously; extend your arms and twist them from side to side. Do you see loose slabs of fat moving beneath the skin? Don't suck in your belly. Don't cheat. Take a long hard merciless look. Acknowledge what is really there. To be objective, imagine that you are looking at a stranger. Is this someone you want to see, to know, to associate with?

Assess your weight distribution, skin condition, muscle tone, posture and grooming. Confront what you see, knowing that this is not an end but a beginning.

Change what you don't like. You have the power to improve the way your presence impacts others. Every improvement gives you added influence. Don't you want to have every possible advantage?

Now stand before the mirror fully dressed. Imagine you are looking at someone else. Don't laugh, this is important. Imagine meeting this person for the first time. What impression do you make? Will this image win the confidence of strangers? Is it the image of a successful person, a person of means—an effective, confident person? Would you feel secure letting this person handle your affairs? Your body and clothing are your interface to the outer world of strangers. Does this image support your dream of success?

Don't make physical appearance an end in itself. Those who trim and train their bodies for sheer vanity alone, without the goals of physical health and oneness of mind and spirit, are racing into a dead end. They are like squirrels on a treadmill, going nowhere at high speed. If you choose to reshape your body, do it as part of a balanced effort.

Analyze your image and reconstruct it from head to foot. The body is relatively easy to bring under your control and therefore the logical place to begin to develop discipline. The results will help train your mind and strengthen the spirit.

Remember this ...

- Your body and clothing are your interface with the world.

- How your appearance impacts others is your business.

- Make the body the first focus of self-discipline.

Try this ...

Think of a person whose general appearance you find consistently admirable and appropriate. Observe that person to discover the choices and habits that produce such impressive results. If possible, ask polite questions to learn more details. Modify and apply some of these tips to the creation of your own image.

24

Skillfully Exercise Emotive Influence

"Acting is all about honesty. If you can fake that, you've got it made."
—George Burns

To emote means to express emotion, often in a rhetorical or dramatic way. Your "emotive impact" refers to your emotional demeanor, the fluid succession of feelings that plays across your face, straightens or slumps your posture and energizes your movements and gestures.

Emotions telegraph intent and a readiness to act. We typically don't expect much from a person who comes across as flat or bland, but we anticipate great things from one who is animated with passion and enthusiasm. When we attempt to read the mood of another person, we look for signs of emotion. And when emotions hold sway over reason, it doesn't much matter how smart we are, we will follow our feelings to ridiculous ends.

We learn to role-play when we are children. As an infant, you studied the faces of people around you and learned their codes of expression. Caregivers trained you to express pleasure, distress, sympathy and love through preverbal communications using facial expressions and body language.

As an adult, your emotive appearance is how you "come off" to others—whether confident, shy, bold, modest, warm, aloof, aggressive, defensive, friendly, or antagonistic. You can allow your demeanor to be as it may, or you can learn to control it with the discipline of an actor.

Skillful actors are convincing in their roles. We feel their sincerity and passion. Their performances reach out and connect with us emotionally. Dedicated actors create their characters from the inside out. Some devote months to researching a role, understanding how the character thinks and feels, living in the same environment and interacting with similar people. Phillip Seymour Hoffman "became" Truman Capote for the film, *Capote*, mimicking the author's voice and mannerisms between as well as during takes. His performance won an academy award.

The rest of us often do the same thing and, in our own way, are just as convincing. It's not a bad thing to assume the qualities of the person you want to be. You can dress like a million in clothes from a resale boutique, speak authoritatively about the things you understand, enter a room as though your arrival were highly anticipated. You can secretly choose an archetype, study the person carefully and then incorporate aspects of his or her style in your own repertoire. Your borrowed persona will invoke reactions from others. Pay attention and adjust accordingly.

There are limits to role playing. Don't compromise your ethics or financial health. Don't be overtly dishonest, phony or pretentious, don't lease a Mercedes on a Saturn budget and, above all, don't lose yourself in the portrayal.

I'm reminded of a man who attempted to model himself after a well-known motivational speaker. He mastered the breezy walk, the open gestures and the unceasing positive attitude, but he missed the humanness. It could be flooding outside and he'd insist the weather was wonderfully refreshing. He had no empathy for other people's worries or concerns because he was too busy being cheerful. Some people learned to avoid him completely. Others found ways to politely excuse themselves when they could no longer tolerate his fraudulent optimism.

Summon the emotion you want to project before attempting to project it. Feel the import of statements before you make them. For example, if you hope to convince someone to try a particular product, take a moment to reexperience the satisfaction you felt when you used the product yourself. Then channel that pleasure and enthusiasm into your eyes, your smile, and the inflection and tone of your voice. Prepare for each encounter as if it were the most important of your life. Your impact upon others will radically influence the speed at which you achieve your goals.

Remember this ...

• Learn to control your emotional demeanor.

• Create the persona you wish to project.

• Avoid dishonesty and pretentiousness.

• Endow communications with emotional authenticity.

Try this ...

Turn off the sound while watching a DVD of a movie (preferably a drama) that you have not previously seen. Pay close attention to the facial expressions and body language of the actors and keep a running list of the emotions portrayed in each major scene. Then go back and watch the same scenes with the sound turned on. How accurate were your observations? (To shorten this exercise, use the scene selector to skip from scene to scene, watching each one just long enough to assess its emotional content.)

25

Effectively Manage Your Time

"The one who rushes ahead hastily will probably fall behind."
—*Chinese Proverb*

Time is the great equalizer, the universal life limiter. Everyone gets 24 hours a day, seven days a week, no more and no less. Time doesn't discriminate. It walks silently beside each of us, an invisible companion to the powerful and underprivileged alike.

Some people do more in a year than others do in a lifetime. How are such differences in leverage possible? Efficiency, that's how. Highly effective individuals learn how to produce results with a minimum of waste, expense and unnecessary effort.

Some people prefer a more leisurely approach to life. They move slowly and waste time here and there throughout the day. If that's your style and you are satisfied with it, learn to accept the lower levels of achievement it earns. Go ahead and enjoy frivolous diversions, but don't use them as excuses. You are choosing leisure time over productivity time. If, on the other hand, you would like to improve your efficiency through better use of time, start by seeking balance.

Here's a simple formula for a balanced life: 8 + 8 + 8. Eight hours of work, eight hours of sleep and eight hours of personal time. Without becoming impossibly rigid, try to apportion your activities accordingly.

The push to get ahead professionally drives many people to work up to sixteen-hour days. Workaholics pay a heavy price for such myopic devotion, in crumbling marriages, resentful children, neglected hobbies, deteriorating friendships and lack of fitness. If sleep is habitually sacrificed, the brain's ability to comprehend, recall, reason and problem solve drops precipitously.

Every afternoon before leaving work, write down the things you intend to accomplish the next day. Challenge yourself, but at the same time be realistic. Prioritize, eliminating or reducing the time allotted to low priority tasks. Never waste precious minutes on senseless minutia. Work a full day and at the end of that time, get up and go home—or to the gym, or your daughter's soccer game, or a dinner party with friends. Wind up evening activities in plenty of time to get a good night's sleep. It takes discipline to consistently achieve this kind of balance, but the effort pays big dividends.

Conduct your own personal time study. Chart a typical week or month. Create a spreadsheet showing how the time was spent. If you are completely honest, the results will be very revealing. The waste in your work days will become immediately evident: unnecessary e-mail and phone calls, Internet browsing, extended coffee breaks, failure to delegate, meetings that don't start or end on time, messy desk, lack of proper tools, coworker interruptions. The list of potential time-wasters is long and infamous. When you know what yours are, start to reduce or eliminate them. Turn off your phone, send and answer e-mail at specific times, close your Internet window, shut your office door, take a day to clean and properly supply your work area, and so on.

Occasionally re-inventory an entire day. Log the time wasted and the time well-spent in your personal as well as professional life. Keep a chart and evaluate the quality of every effort and activity. Isolate and identify personal time-wasters. To maximize efficiency, eliminate such things as moronic television shows and pointless trips to the mall.

Identify healthful non-work activities, such as sports, volunteer work and quality time with family and loved ones. Healthful off-duty periods contribute to your productivity. Your subconscious mind continues to work during satisfying recreation.

Avoid distractions when focusing on important tasks and events. Choose quality over quantity. An hour of concentrated work is worth three hours of stops, starts and interruptions. The same is true for family and loved ones. Ten minutes of thoughtful conversation are far more valuable than an hour of shared "American Idol" mania.

Never rush when working on priority issues, but develop the ability to multi-task routine duties—things you know by rote. A word of caution: research has demonstrated that multi-tasking produces poorer results on all tasks simultaneously undertaken than on those same tasks handled one at a time. For example, many people drive while participating in telephonic meetings and issuing remote managerial guidance. Neither the driving nor the interactions receive full attention so quality drops and mistakes (including traffic mishaps) rise. Save multi-tasking for mostly mindless duties, which by definition never happen behind the wheel of a car unless it is parked.

The amount of time required for a task and the quality achieved are largely functions of your ability to focus. Focus is the full concentration of your attention on the job at hand. It requires letting go of everything outside the precise dimensions of the task, often including time itself. People with a well developed ability to focus may need to set an alarm in order to break their concentration and end each work session on time.

As you become more efficient and streamlined at managing your time, you will build faith in your decision-making ability, which will in turn accelerate your actions and create even greater efficiency. This is the continuous self-reinforcing cycle to which you must aspire.

Remember this ...

• Seek balance: 8 plus 8 plus 8.

• Identify and eliminate time-wasters.

• Quality of time spent is more important than quantity.

• Save multi-tasking for routine duties.

• Give full focus to complex and high priority matters.

Try this ...

Keep a time log for one week. Record all activities in 15 minute increments. At the end of the week, analyze the results. Look for patterns. What are your most prevalent time-wasters? During what hours are you most productive? How can you take advantage of those periods? When do you become listless, distracted, restless or bored? What can you do to minimize or counteract unproductive periods?

26

Use Tasking to Measure Progress

"Things do not change; we change."
—Henry David Thoreau

Rome was not built in a day. Though your dream may now be visible on the horizon, many goals must be met and many steps taken to arrive at that destination. Much of the time the journey will be smooth and stress-free. However, occasionally you will feel overwhelmed by the complexity of a challenging goal, and progress will slow. To help yourself get through the uphill climbs, make it a habit to break down complicated goals into smaller tasks. Keep breaking them down until you can see the first small step, the second small step and so on.

Each evening, create a list of small steps to do the following day. Carry over items from previous days that haven't been completed. When you finish a task, check it off the list. This will build momentum. You must recognize the accomplishment of very small things to be happy on a daily basis.

Think of the scientist who spends months or even years working in the lab to test a given theory. The work is exacting. The tiniest observations are recorded and detailed records are kept. On a regular basis the investigator publishes scientific papers in which he or she shares new information with the rest of the scientific community. To the average outsider, the pace of such work appears snail-like, but to the scientist, who sees implications and spin-offs stretching to infinity, every molecule of progress is vitally important.

Take a lesson from the scientist. Each evening, recap some of the small advances you've made during the day. Once in awhile, take time to look at the cumulative impact of your efforts and measure the distance you've traveled. Keep simple notes, or make daily entries in a journal. Record your thoughts, feelings and observations. These may prove invaluable in the future as a record of your personal growth, changing insights and determination.

Long-range planning in the form of a life map and goals does not in itself deliver a sense of closure. It can take weeks, months or even years to reach a goal. This lack of closure is likely to increase the amount of ambiguity and uncertainty in your life, generating day-to-day frustration. Tasking resolves this dilemma by building in daily feedback and reinforcement. Tasking helps you bridge the gap between where you are now and where you hope to be when your goals have been realized.

Tasking is highly compatible with an action-oriented temperament or style. You cannot *do* a goal, you can only do an activity or task. Focusing on the daily lineup of tasks will satisfy your innate drive to get things done.

Tasking is a valuable tool for the less action-oriented as well. When you develop a list of tasks, you are making a compact with yourself. It's mere existence serves as an inescapable injunction to act.

Few of us have someone in our lives who notices every modicum of progress we make. Personal and executive coaching have become popular in recent years precisely for that reason. Coaches not only recognize and reinforce positive efforts, they help clients sort out priorities, set goals and stay on track. If hiring one of these professional cheerleaders is unrealistic for you, become your own coach.

A coach is an independent monitor. Without independent monitoring, your desire to change may fade and you may slip back into previous behaviors, neglecting goals in the process. To remain entirely independent while monitoring your own efforts is asking the impossible, but discipline yourself to be objective. Change is something that happens through a continuous process of evaluation. If you had a coach, the coach would talk with you weekly, listen carefully, offer ideas, remind you of your goals and congratulate you on your progress. These are the things you must do for yourself.

If you take your progress for granted, you won't be stimulated to take the next step or to set the next required goal. So without losing sight of the big picture, concentrate on tasking.

Remember this ...

• Break down complicated goals into small tasks.

• Recognize the accomplishment of each small thing.

• Continuously monitor and celebrate your progress.

• Every step makes the next step easier.

Try this ...

When tasking a project or goal, be sure to write down each small step. Daily planners often have special pages for this purpose. Electronic devices have similar functions. Or you can just use a sheet of paper. Two important benefits are derived from this process. First, you are less likely to omit an important step. It's simply good planning. Second, you experience the satisfaction of physically crossing out each completed task and watching the list grow smaller and smaller. Don't deny yourself this momentum builder by keeping everything in your head.

27

Cultivate Flexibility

"Nothing endures but change."
—Heraclitus

Almost nothing goes exactly as planned. People get sick and change their minds, companies fail and close, natural disasters strike, conflicts arise, resources dry up—the potential sources of disruption are legion. Even the most thorough planning cannot predict the endless variables that crop up on a given goal path. The more complex a goal—the more variables involved—the greater the chances that some part of your plan will need to be adjusted. To be ready for such moments, temper your drive and determination with a willingness and ability to be flexible. Like an agile boxer, be light on your feet, always ready to punch, duck or dodge.

If you are a good time manager, you already know how to build in allowances for the unexpected. You've learned from experience approximately how much time to reserve for interruptions and crises. With a built-in cushion, you can integrate unplanned activities without disrupting an entire day's schedule. The same approach can be applied in the pursuit of goals. Uncertainty is ever present. No one can know how any venture will turn out. An attitude of flexibility will allow you to shape the unexpected to your needs and use it to enrich, rather than destroy, your vision.

Athletes maintain physical flexibility by regularly stretching their muscles. Stretching literally extends a person's reach—an appropriate metaphor for what it accomplishes in other areas of life as well. Flexibility in the job market means having the knowledge and skills to qualify for a wide range of positions and the willingness to consider them. Flexibility in negotiations means being open to different points of view and willing to collaborate and compromise. Flexibility in marriage can mean sharing domestic chores and decision-making responsibilities with your spouse.

Flexibility is the opposite of rigidity. A rigid person takes a position and refuses to bend under any circumstances, even when the preponderance of evidence points to the need for a course correction. As the weeks and months go by, the path of the rigid person moves further and further from reality—becoming a misguided trip to nowhere.

Don't be alarmed when you have to make adjustments. Don't feel the need to apologize because your original plan didn't work perfectly. Above all, don't be tempted to quit.

Develop resilience— the ability to quickly recover from disappointment, change and misfortune. Flexibility and resilience are closely related. Both require the ability to appraise situations, identify alternative courses of action and make sound decisions. Resilient people are problem-solvers. They take setbacks in stride, and are challenged, not crippled, by change. Resilience has been identified as a key personality trait of at-risk youth who overcome severe social and economic hardships to achieve success in school and life.

Each time you complete a step in your plan, or experience a small success, or solve even a minor problem, your resilience will grow and strengthen. Instead of reacting to change with hesitation and pessimism, you will experience increasing confidence in your ability to prevail over unexpected setbacks and challenging conditions. This sense of mastery over your life will ensure that you learn from mistakes and persistently strive to reach your goals.

Being comfortable with ambiguity and change requires a certain degree of optimism. If the path veers off your expected direction, don't be alarmed. Confidently go where the path takes you. Assess and the new circumstances, make adjustments and take positive action.

Remember this ...

• Few things go exactly as planned.

• Temper determination and drive with flexibility.

• Cultivate resilience.

• Be challenged (not crippled) by change.

• Changing direction does not mean giving up control.

Try this ...

Pick any object in your immediate environment and quickly think of 6 to 10 things that it could be used for other than the purpose for which it was invented. For example, a paper clip can be used as a hairpin, a nail cleaner, an ornament-hanger, a screwdriver, an earring, a toothpick (plastic-covered, please), a bookmark, a hinge-screw for eyeglasses, an emergency disk-drive ejector, and, when linked with others, a bracelet. This is a fun game to play while sitting around a table with friends. Quickly pass an object (a fork, for instance) from person to person. Each person must think of a new use for the object before passing it to the next person.

Forgive Yourself

> *"And when I was born I drew in the common air, and fell upon the earth, which is of like nature; and the first voice I uttered was crying, as all others do."*
> —*The Wisdom of Solomon*

Don't be weighed down by regret over past mistakes and inadequacies. If you are disappointed in yourself, if you feel you have failed in the past, an attitude of unworthiness will affect everything you do. Get rid of all pent-up discontent. Look deep within yourself, inventory the regrets and failures of the past, systematically own up to them and then forgive yourself for each and every one. Be your own confessor. Impose penance if you think it will help. For example, if you owe someone money, repay it with interest. If you owe someone an apology, sincerely give it. Then, once and for all, absolve yourself of guilt and get on with your journey.

What are you holding against yourself? Why do you beat yourself up? Forgive yourself for all the personal felonies that confine your spirit to a prison of self-loathing.

Forgive yourself for being old. It's never too late to start a new career, begin a new relationship, take up a new hobby or learn a new skill. If you are older, you have the advantage of life experience and bring years of accumulated knowledge to every pursuit. Cosmetic surgery and youthful attire not withstanding, there's little you can do about the march of time, so accept your age and rejoice in the advantages it gives you.

Forgive yourself for neglecting your talents. Maybe you feel as though you should apologize for your lack of achievement up to this point in life. When you look around, your peers all seem to have more income, bigger houses, fancier cars, more exotic vacations. You can't think of any convincing excuses for not having the same, so you blame yourself—like the woman who ran into a classmate from high school and was stunned to discover all the things he had accomplished in the 20 years since they'd last seen each other. By comparison, her life seemed mundane, her accomplishments insignificant. She felt as though she had been asleep under a rock for two decades. But she was mistaken. She had raised two children and held responsible jobs. Still young, her future was wide open.

Forgive yourself for being imperfect. Don't hold yourself to unreasonable standards of excellence. Perfectionism sets the stage for continuous disappointment and, in some cases, psychic paralysis. Perfectionists often hesitate to try new things for fear of turning in less than a topnotch performance. It's okay to be second best, so relax. Know when to stop fine-tuning an endeavor and move on to the next project. Give yourself permission to be human.

Forgive yourself for being young. It's never too early to develop a vision of the life you want to lead and begin the journey to your goals. If the people around you are older and more experienced, learn from them, but don't be intimidated by them.

Forgive yourself for your roots. Whether you come from wealth or poverty, education or ignorance, from farmers, merchants, soldiers or slaves does not predispose you to a particular level in life unless you let it. If you didn't have advantages growing up, you might have to work a little harder, but that's nothing to be ashamed of. Your legacy carries many positive lessons. Embrace them.

Look into your heart and forgive the flaws you see. Start fresh. Consider yourself raw material, ready to be shaped anew.

The past can never be changed, but the future is yours. Your dream awaits you. Let the future begin.

Remember this ...

- Regardless of your age, today is the first day of the rest of your life. Make it count.

- It's never too late to develop a neglected talent.

- Excellence is always possible, perfection rarely is.

- Don't be slowed by ruts in the road behind you.

Try this ...

List your losses as far back as you can remember—all the way to early childhood. Release the grief by hitting a chair with a rolled-up towel, having a temper tantrum on your bed, pounding a board with a hammer, or hitting a punching bag. Cry till you are no longer sad and pound till you are no longer mad about the loss. Forgive yourself and others.

29

Connect and Communicate

"The character of a man is known from his conversations."
—Menander

More often than not, successful people are social animals who thrive on the energy derived from successful interpersonal relations—from making meaningful professional and social connections with other people.

Effective interactions are built on good communication—the ability to listen attentively, express your ideas clearly, participate effectively in group discussions and handle yourself well in social settings, negotiations and conflicts. What are your communication strengths and weaknesses? What skills do you need to acquire or improve?

Listening is arguably the most important, and most neglected, communication skill. You can be a supremely eloquent speaker and still fail to communicate if you refuse to close your mouth occasionally and hear what others have to say. Poor listeners get directions and instructions wrong, misunderstand ideas, jump to faulty conclusions and give the impression they don't care what others think. In contrast, good listeners demonstrate interest and respect by not interrupting. They concentrate on what is being said rather than what they plan to say next.

Good listeners ask for clarification if they don't understand something and are patient when people have trouble expressing themselves. They summarize what they have heard to check the accuracy of their interpretations. If your listening skills need to be remedied, pick one behavior at a time and practice it. For example, spend a day (or, better, a week) biting your tongue every time you start to interrupt someone.

Public speaking has long been the number one fear of Americans—scarier than snakes and spiders, more terrifying than terrorists. If this is an area of trepidation for you, start slowly to develop your speaking skills. Begin by conveying relatively simple thoughts in a well-conceived manner. Think about what you are going to say, choose your words carefully, speak in complete sentences and express emotion. Convey enthusiasm, skepticism, puzzlement—whatever you are feeling—in your facial expressions and tone of voice. As you feel more comfortable speaking, increase your "floor time" until you feel ready to give an entire report or presentation.

Use the same approach in meetings, work teams and small gatherings. Groups often provide ideal conditions in which to develop speaking skills. Don't let shyness inhibit you from contributing. Develop confidence in your convictions. If your beliefs are in the minority, don't assume that no one wants to hear them. Groups benefit from a diversity of ideas and viewpoints. Imagine the consequences when a member of a governing board votes in favor of an action even though she secretly opposes it. Not only is the decision automatically weakened by her hidden opposition, the entire group is deprived of her viewpoint, which might be critically valuable. In the movie *Twelve Angry Men*, the Henry Fonda character gradually sways an entire jury through persistent inquiry and quiet determination.

You say as much or more with facial expressions and body language as you do with words, so aim for congruence between verbal and nonverbal communication. If you laugh while expressing dissatisfaction, or sigh and moan while claiming to be "fine," you are sending a mixed message. Mixed messages confuse people and undermine trust. If you fold up like a flower at sunset when speaking before a group, your message, too, will fade.

Allow your body language to reinforce everything you say—in simple conversations, in business dealings and in formal presentations.

When you disagree with people, try to appreciate why they believe as they do. Understand their thoughts before you throw away their ideas. Balance persuasive argument with good listening. Seek common ground and build consensus.

When you have an important message to deliver and others are unwilling to listen, keep trying. Each effort will enlarge your sense of what reaches people and what fails to engage them. These efforts build muscle in your speaking and social skills.

Finally, cultivate a genuine interest in other people. Show your sincere desire to connect with them by initiating conversations and asking questions about their activities, ideas and opinions. One of the best ways to spot an interested person is by counting follow-up questions. A person who is just going through the motions typically runs out of curiosity very quickly. For example, when Joe asks Paul, "What did you do yesterday?" and Paul answers, "I spent the day at the park," Joe will say, "I thought about going to the park, but it was too cold, so I went and saw this great movie, which is all about..." and carry on about the movie, completely forgetting that the conversation started with an inquiry into Paul's activities. In contrast, when Ivan asks, "What did you do yesterday?" and Paul answers, "I spent the day at the park," Ivan will probe, "Which park did you go to?" and "What did you do at the park?" and "Who went with you?" and "What was the weather like?" Ivan keeps asking questions because he has a genuine interest in Paul and his activities.

Think about the best communicators you know and the leaders you admire. How do they interact with others? What admired traits can you emulate?

Decide to improve your skills in one area at a time. Begin a program of self-monitoring in that area only. Don't be afraid to correct mistakes and rephrase statements, even in the middle of a conversation. The other person will understand if you explain that you are attempting to become a better communicator.

Remember this ...

- Good relationships are built on good communication.

- To get the facts straight, listen.

- To understand the views and ideas of others, listen.

- To demonstrate respect and caring, listen.

- Before you speak, think.

- Match verbal language with body language.

- When important ideas are received poorly or not at all, keep trying.

- Cultivate a genuine interest in other people.

Try this ...

When you want to stimulate discussion or conversation, ask open-ended questions—questions that cannot be answered "yes" or "no." For example, ask, "What are your views about ..." or "What is the most important thing you learned from ..." Then listen.

30

Believe in Yourself

"It is possible to fail in many ways…while to succeed is possible only in one way."
—Aristotle

Society imposes limits on people based on race, culture, background, education and wealth. But these limits are never impenetrable. In free societies, people frequently outdistance conventional expectations. The son of a postal worker graduates from Harvard. The daughter of a mechanic builds a million-dollar business. How do they do it? Every story is different, but amid the variables you will find at least one common denominator: successful people believe in themselves.

The only cast iron limitations are the ones you impose on yourself. You can never be more than what you believe you can be, so work first on your own belief system. Break the knee-jerk habit of thinking and saying, "I can't," in the face of challenging opportunities. It's been said that success is what happens when preparation meets opportunity, and a big part of preparation is disciplining your mind to eliminate self-defeating thoughts.

Some people are enthusiastic starters, but fade in the backstretch. Lacking stamina and endurance, they are ill-prepared for the long race. A setback or two sends them limping to the sidelines. How often have you heard, "I'll try it for a month," or "I'll give it a year and see what happens"? Such people begin their journey with one foot already off the path. They are ready to stray, to slow, to meander, to change course before they even start. They begin with defeat built into their mindset.

If you have a history of quitting, please understand this brutally simple axiom: quitting is an option only for the defeated.

Refuse to accept this weak mindset. Believe you can succeed. Release yourself from the fears that pollute your thinking and stay your actions. Few goals worth pursuing are easy to achieve, so keep at it, believe in yourself, and your chances for a high-achieving future will flourish.

Create a solid foundation for your dream and pursue each goal with enthusiasm and quiet conviction. Determine basic requirements that must be met to build the future you believe essential. Begin every day working toward that dream, brick by brick. Go to sleep every night examining your progress and planning for the next day's campaign to seize the building blocks needed to finish the dream and make it real.

Remember this ...

• The only limitations are those you impose on yourself.

• Eliminate self-defeating thoughts.

• Quitting is an option only for the defeated.

• Believe in yourself.

Try this ...

Reread sections of this book regularly. Review the summary pages and add notes and ideas of your own. Keep track of your progress in a log or diary. Write the story of your success one day at a time.

At the ripe old age of 30, Hart Cunningham has already launched dozens of highly successful solely-owned businesses, without venture capital.

Cunningham's life has been rich with learning challenges, from college baseball to an MBA at 22, selling Wall Street corporations at 23 and launching his first global company at 24, followed by dozens more to date. His companies have been praised in hundreds of publications, from *Wall Street Review* to *Time Magazine* to the *New York Times*.

The Organizational Zoo

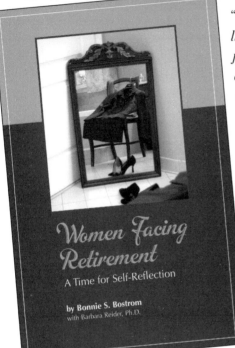

Surviving Breast Cancer

Foot Soldiers
Stories From The Breast Cancer 3-Day Walk

by Deborah Douglas, M.D.
With foreword by David W. Lounsbury, Ph.D.,
Memorial Sloan-Kettering Cancer Center

Retired pathologist, author, and breast cancer survivor, Deborah Douglas, M.D., walked 600 miles in 10 Breast Cancer 3-Day events to interview cancer survivors and co-survivors. The collected stories not only emphasize the complexity of diagnosis, treatment, and survivorship, but—due in large part to the emotional honesty of the contributors—challenge the popular mantras that a positive attitude is the only healthy way to cope with the disease and that cancer is an unequivocal gift.

Read this book if you are:

- **A cancer patient or loved one who wants to know how other patients handle the challenges of diagnosis, treatment, and survivorship and still find the courage to participate in a long-distance walk**

- **A health-care provider who wants cancer patients to understand that there are no right or wrong ways to face this disease**

- **Interested in signing up for a Breast Cancer 3-Day event, but want to know what it's really like to walk 60 miles, sleep in a tent, shower in a truck, and use porta-potties**

- **Simply curious why an otherwise perfectly reasonable middle-aged woman would leave behind her comfortable home, family, friends, and dogs to walk 600 miles in 10 cities**

The chapters deftly weave together incidents, observations, and conversations from the walks themselves; the stories of survivors and their families; the medical "journeys" of those survivors along with accessible technical explanations; and occasional incidents and insights from the author's own story. The writing is technically excellent, compassionate, humorous, and emotionally open. Everything about this book is exemplary.

—Dianne Schilling, Instructional Designer

ISBN: 0944031 24 2

www.AslanPublishing.com • www.the3-daybook.com
Available nationally at bookstores and online webstores

Aslan
PUBLISHING

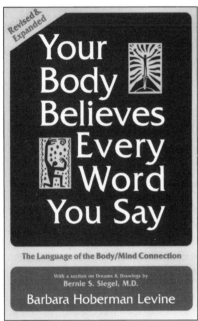